"Matousek's book resurrects an Emerson who was writing to be heard."

—*The Wall Street Journal*

"This beautifully written book on Emerson offers great principles and notions for living through these difficult times. It restored my enthusiasm, confidence, compassion, and willingness to resist authority. It made me braver to be myself, to embrace paradox, and be proud of all the ways I have refused to conform. It's a guide for living outside binaries. It's a book of great vitality, vision, and liberation."

—V (formerly Eve Ensler), author of *Reckoning*

"If Ralph Waldo Emerson were alive today, he'd be exactly the man for our times—spiritually independent, psychologically savvy, and full of the common sense we need to infuse our culture with wisdom and moral courage. I am so grateful to Mark Matousek for this user-friendly book and for diving deep into Emerson's works. I keep the book on my bedside table and dip into it whenever my heart needs a lift."

—Elizabeth Lesser, author of the *New York Times* bestseller *Broken Open*

"It is a filial love story, a profound appreciation of Ralph Waldo Emerson's great mind and spirit. This is not only a touching account of the work of a great man by whom too many people today are intimidated, but also a narrative of achieving intimacy with ideas, thoughts, and feelings that had been absent from Matousek's lived experience."

—Andrew Solomon, author of *The Noonday Demon* and *Far from the Tree*

"In this compelling exploration applying deep wisdom to everyday life, Matousek has masterfully curated a way to live with more freedom, connection, and meaning in our lives. Weaving fascinating stories about Ralph Waldo Emerson, personal accounts, and the ancient perspective of Stoicism, this journey will invite you to get to know three individuals in a powerful way—Waldo, Matousek, and yourself—opening your mind to helpful insights and new ways of living in our challenging world. A fascinating and helpful historical review as current today as it is universal in its applications across time."

—Daniel J. Siegel, MD, *New York Times* bestselling author of *IntracConnected*, *Mindsight*, and *Aware*

"In *Lessons from an American Stoic*, Matousek is more than an outstanding biographer of the legendary Emerson. He joins the lineage of Emerson by adding his own hard-earned wisdom and care. In translating Emerson's insights to our modern world, Mark has done a great service for the soul of America. This is a great book. It will open your heart, expand your mind, and help you live more truly, more fully, and more lovingly."

—Mark Nepo, author of *The Half-Life of Angels* and *Falling Down and Getting Up*

"Emerson's spirit is exactly what we need to recognize now in our broken country community. I will sing the praises of him, and this book, to everyone I know."

—Marie Howe, author of *What the Living Do*

"Through the crystalline clarity of his writing, Matousek has managed to make Emerson utterly accessible to all of us. This is must-reading for Emerson lovers and anyone looking for deep-rooted wisdom to accompany their life journey."

—Gail Straub, author of *Women and Water*

"This book is a master class in Emerson, and Mark Matousek is your ideal companion to the timeless and transformative insights of America's premier thinker. *Lessons from an American Stoic* showed me a new way of looking at my life, and how I might live it more profoundly if I allowed the wisdom of Emerson to guide me."

—Rabbi Rami Shapiro, author of *Holy Rascals: Advice for Spiritual Revolutionaries*

"I have been guided by Emerson's essays and journals for decades, and I'm always astonished by his fresh way of imagining human life and his original way of putting his ideas into words. Mark Matousek's soft and fluid language is perfect for introducing you to Emerson or reminding you to read him again. This is a beautiful book, full of ideas that could help restore America's genius for freedom and promise."

—Thomas Moore, *New York Times* bestselling author of *Care of the Soul*

Emerson,
the Stoics,
and Me

ALSO BY MARK MATOUSEK

Writing to Awaken: A Journey of Truth, Transformation, and Self-Discovery

Sex Death Enlightenment: A True Story

The Boy He Left Behind: A Man's Search for His Lost Father

When You're Falling, Dive: Lessons in the Art of Living

Ethical Wisdom: The Search for a Moral Life

Mother of the Unseen World: The Mystery of Mother Meera

Ethical Wisdom for Friends

Emerson, the Stoics, and Me

Timeless Wisdom for Living an Authentic Life

PREVIOUSLY PUBLISHED AS
LESSONS FROM AN AMERICAN STOIC

Mark Matousek

HarperOne

An Imprint of HarperCollinsPublishers

HarperCollins books may be purchased for educational, business, or sales promotional use. For information, please email the Special Markets Department at SPsales@harpercollins.com.

FIRST HARPERCOLLINS PAPERBACK EDITION PUBLISHED IN 2025

Designed by Ralph Fowler

Library of Congress Cataloging-in-Publication Data is available upon request.

ISBN 978-0-06-305970-2

25 26 27 28 29 LBC 5 4 3 2 1

To David and Joy

The unfolding of his nature is the chief end of man.

—R.W.E.

Sometimes even to live is an act of courage.

—Seneca

CONTENTS

KEY TO ABBREVIATIONS

Throughout the text, I've used abbreviations to reference quotations taken from Emerson's public lectures and essays. Many of these quotes are widely known and easy to find, and my favorite go-to sources are included in the bibliography. Quotations from Emerson's dedication speeches and valedictory events are referenced in detail below. All material quoted from Waldo's miscellaneous private writing and journals is identified with standard endnotes in the notes section.

AOE Address on Education (published posthumously in *The Complete Writings of Ralph Waldo Emerson*, edited by his son, Edward Emerson, in 1904)

B "Beauty" (*The Conduct of Life*, 1860)

C "Compensation" (*Essays, First Series*, 1841)

CBW "Considerations by the Way" (*The Conduct of Life*, 1860)

CFL Address at the Concord Free Library (1835)

CHA "Character" (*Essays, Second Series*, 1844)

CIR   "Circles" (*Essays, First Series*, 1841)

CL   "Clubs" (*Society and Solitude*, 1870)

COI   Celebration of Intellect Speech at Tufts College (1861)

CON   "The Conservative" (lecture at the Masonic Temple, 1841)

CONS   "Considerations" (*The Conduct of Life*, 1860)

COU   "Courage" (*Society and Solitude*, 1870)

CTH   Speech for Meeting of the Citizens Town Hall, Concord (1856)

CUL   "Culture" (*The Conduct of Life*, 1860)

DSA   Harvard Divinity School Address (1838)

E   "Experience" (*Essays, Second Series*, 1844)

F   "Fate" (*The Conduct of Life*, 1860)

FR   "Friendship" (*Essays, First Series*, 1841)

FSL   Fugitive Slave Law Speech (address to Citizens of Concord, 1851)

H   "History" (*Essays, First Series*, 1841)

INS   "Inspiration" (*Letters and Social Aims*, 1875)

INT   "Intellect" (*Essays, First Series*, 1841)

L   "Love" (*Essays, First Series*, 1841)

M   "Manners" (*Essays, Second Series*, 1844)

MON   "Montaigne; or, The Skeptic" (*Representative Men*, 1850)

MTR   "Man the Reformer" (lecture read before the Mechanics' Apprentices' Library Association, 1841)

N   "Nature" (*Nature*, 1836)

NHI   "Natural History of the Intellect" (*The Conduct of Life*, 1860)

O   "The Over-Soul" (*Essays, First Series*, 1841)

POL   "Politics" (*The Conduct of Life*, 1860)

POW   "Power" (*The Conduct of Life*, 1860)

S   "Success" (*Society and Solitude*, 1870)

SL   "Spiritual Laws" (*Essays, First Series*, 1841)

SR   "Self-Reliance" (*Essays, First Series*, 1841)

T   "The Transcendentalist" (lecture read at the Masonic Temple, 1842)

TAS   "The American Scholar" (Phi Beta Kappa speech, 1837)

TT   "The Tragic" (essay from *The Dial*, 1844)

TYA   "The Young American" (lecture read before the Mercantile Library Association, 1844)

W   "Worship" (*The Conduct of Life*, 1860)

WAD   "Work and Days" (*Society and Solitude*, 1870)

WCS   Williams College Speech (1854)

Falling in Love with Emerson

I first fell in love with Ralph Waldo Emerson at a crisis point in my own life. I was a heartsick twenty-two-year-old graduate student, floundering in academia, panicky about my future, over-whelmed by self-doubt, and terrified I would never discover who I was—really—or why I'd been put on this baffling planet.

I'd struggled with confusion since childhood. Everywhere I turned, duplicity and hypocrisy were obvious to me as a boy. Nothing—and no one—was quite what it appeared to be. The grown-ups juggled alternating masks in different surroundings and I was a two-faced deceiver myself, concealing who I really was—an angry, fatherless, damaged boy—under a shield of Teflon bravado. I acted the part of an all-American overachiever with a promising future ahead of him while inwardly I was a miserable train wreck—cynical, paranoid, lonely, and lost. I told myself that an advanced degree would help to boost my drooping self-esteem, but that was a fantasy. When that fall semester started, I was as frustrated, angry, and self-punishing as I had ever been in my life, suffocating in academia, bereft of inspiration, holding my breath—hoping for something important to happen, to make things matter, to give me a purpose. Yet what that elusive thing was, exactly, I could not say.

I was also chronically out of cash, which is what led me to apply for a research assistant's job working for a visiting professor from Yale named Barbara Packer. Professor Packer needed a flunky to do the grunt work on a manuscript she was late in delivering, a study of Ralph Waldo Emerson's major essays. My job was to hunt down out-of-print reference books, excavate ancient newspaper clips, and transcribe notes from blurry microfiches onto multicolored three-by-five index cards. I knew very little about Emerson at the time. I'd read snippets of his extravagant prose in high school but mostly remembered him as the avuncular mentor to the younger, hipper, more tragic Henry David Thoreau, whose *Walden* had wowed many of us in senior English. Professor Packer kept me on my toes that year, poring through the library stacks, lugging books home to compare to textual references, and by the time that spring semester rolled around, I'd managed to receive—with no forethought on my part—a fairly good introduction to the life and works of this extraordinary man.

Meeting Emerson changed my life. His big ideas challenged my puny worldview and exposed me to a vision of human potential I had never known existed. His insights were radical and paradigm-shifting: human life has a spiritual purpose (to recognize our true nature, evolve from ignorance to self-knowledge); we are each endowed with unique purpose and genius, and our mandate is to unfold our character as passionately, originally, and bravely as possible. Emerson taught that pain, loss, suffering, and conflict are teachers and guides in disguise, crucial for our awakening; and that nonconformity, inconsistency, introversion, stubbornness, quirkiness, and a "little wickedness" are beneficial virtues for self-realization. Following the crowd is a mistake, and changing your mind is a very good thing. These were eye-opening insights for me, opposed to everything I had been taught. The idea that we are spiritual beings first, personalities second, that no real separation exists between human life and God, cast a sacred light on existence that I had never seen before.

In the secular America where I'd grown up, God was off-limits as a serious topic. I had no faith in a divine creator, was opposed to most organized religions, and considered myself a firm agnostic. Yet when Emerson counseled, "You look within not to find yourself but to find God,"[1] I had a sense of what he meant though the terminology was arcane and loaded. When he described the One Mind, the divine intelligence, running like an electric cord through creation, he spoke deeply to my unarticulated experience. He taught that Nature is God made visible in the world—that we see God through the mirror of nature, in other words—and that we are reflected in the creation. He explained that genius is the light of divine intelligence within us, and that we're inseparable from this power source; that happiness results from obeying its guidance, trusting our own choices, resisting the urge to imitate, knowing ourselves as outcroppings of the natural world (and, therefore, of God), joined in a kind of cosmic fandango with all of existence.

The more of Emerson I read, the more alive I felt. I began to make overdue decisions. I left graduate school, made amends with my family, broke off a bad relationship, moved to New York City, started finding work as a freelance journalist, and stopped blaming the world for my problems. My addiction to taking offense over tiny social transgressions finally lost its allure. "Never fall into the vulgar mistake of dreaming that [you are] persecuted when [you are] contradicted," Emerson warns us.[2] I could hear him speaking to me. I focused on looking inside for the source of my troubles, examining my "angle of vision," the stories I told myself *about* myself and the world: who I took myself to be, what things signified, the details that mattered, and those that did not. Emerson emphasized that your angle of vision creates your world, an insight he shared with the ancient Stoics, and that genuine freedom rests in the power to choose how we wish to respond to life's conditions. Knowing that perspective shapes reality, we're better able to interrupt our knee-jerk reactions and respond to challenges more skillfully, constructively, mindfully. Except in rare cases of affliction—under physical torture or sickness, for example—a person always has the power to choose her responses and decide when, how, and by whom (or what) she allows herself to be hurt. It was glaringly obvious that the majority of my problems were self-created and arose from how I was choosing to look at situations, not from the circumstances themselves. I learned from Emerson that it is the tendency to cling to false beliefs, and confuse our narratives for reality, that gives rise to most of our suffering. Self-hating, dishonest, twisted stories diminish our lives and prevent us from knowing who we are. Robbed of self-knowledge, we lose our direction. "If one does not know to which port one is sailing, no wind is favorable," Seneca reminded us.[3] A firm grasp on your compass is necessary to reach the desired shore.

My own lifeboat capsized again two years after I arrived in New York. I received a fatal diagnosis that promised me no more than five years to live. With mortality in my face, all bets were off: I quit my vapid magazine job, sold my belongings, gave up the lease on my apartment, said goodbye to my friends, and traveled with a friend to India in hopes of finding a spiritual path that would help me survive my mortal terror. I hopped around from monasteries to ashrams to healing workshops, overwhelmed with questions, seeking spiritual strength, clawing my way through an encroaching darkness. My shredded copy of *The Portable Emerson* was always with me. If I was having a particularly gruesome day, a well-spent hour with Emerson could pull me off the ledge, remind me of possibility, settle my nerves, shift my perspective, and loosen the noose of self-pity I struggled to keep from around my neck. By the mid-1990s, strangely enough, I was still around and reasonably healthy, and when treatments for my condition finally appeared, I was given a second lease on life, surreal and surprising in the extreme. Aristotle compared good luck to the moment on a battlefield when the arrow hits the guy next to you. It's an abstract, outer-space, torn-in-half emotion, partly shattering, partly sublime. Awe is the only word that fits.

This torn-in-half feeling of tenuous survival is akin to how many are feeling today. As the world has become more unhinged, a collective sense of outrage and disbelief has settled over citizens in countries around the world, a kind of post-traumatic shock, paranoia, exhaustion, mistrust, and dread of the next heart-stopping news. There's a dire need for spiritual direction, justice-seeking, restitution, truth-telling, and repairing of the social fabric. Fortunately, alongside this collective trauma is a growing interest in our own potential, an urgent pull toward awakening, a fierce determination to learn from calamity, question our values, reshape our choices, optimize our potential, and cherish our lives, knowing how quickly they can be threatened or taken from us completely. The pandemic has bequeathed us (along with some terrible things) a sudden planetary awareness of our shared impermanence and fragility. This global collision with mortality has given rise to a proportionate upsurge of public interest in self-examination, authenticity, identity, purpose, and what it means to be a fully human being. Not since the consciousness revolution of the 1960s have we witnessed such a nations-wide display of soul-searching and spiritual hunger as we see now.

That is my purpose for writing this book. Emerson's trans-formational wisdom is exactly the medicine we need today. His teaching shows us that there is a way through—even when all can seem lost—a humanistic path to self-knowledge that combines the pragmatic, unsentimental strength of the Stoics with the majesty, beauty, and freedom of Transcendental philosophy. Having used these lessons for forty years, I can attest to their power and usefulness and their profound relevance to the problems we face as contemporary people. Emerson will teach you, if you let him, to break down the walls of perceived limitations, move beyond the confines of the self-absorbed ego, and attain a vision of your life that is infinitely larger, deeper, and richer than anything you believed possible. "The health of the eye [demands] a horizon. We are never tired, so long as we can see far enough," he tells us (*N*). May this book be a helpmeet in seeing farther, standing taller, listening more closely, loving more deeply, and savoring without apology or reservation the preciousness of your life. Emerson is the teacher we need today. It is high time we reclaimed our national treasure.

Trust Yourself

Dangerous times call for life-saving measures. When human survival is under threat, when our highest values are in decline, we require the sturdiest rope to cling to, a time-tested body of practical wisdom with which to steady ourselves through threat and upheaval.

During the most polarizing, violent period in our nation's history, from pre-Abolition through the Civil War, an ex-minister named Ralph Waldo Emerson rallied his fellow Americans to trust the better angels of their nature and not be defeated by despair. He called on them to remember their boundless potential, the spirit of ingenuity, audacity, and freedom latent inside them when and *if* they learned to trust themselves. Emerson was this country's founding philosopher, the Oracle of Concord, the spiritual guide of a fledgling nation in search of its transcendental soul. His influence on our national character is so pervasive that it often escapes our attention. *Do your own thing. Follow your bliss. Life is a journey, not a destination.* All of these come from Emerson. Our core belief in the inalienable right to choose our own way, exceed expectations, fulfill our own potential, rise on the basis of merit, and maintain a private self, immune to the pressures of society—these seminal American values come directly from his particular vision of how self-aware human beings can live.

In his lectures, essays, criticism, poems, and letters, Emerson became the eloquent voice of America's conscience for more than half a century. The spiritual path he called self-reliance promises that everyone is capable of transcending the limitations of her birth regardless of her skin color, class, financial status, or social obstacles. Emerson believed that a spiritual incandescence shines within the human heart and brightens as our self-knowledge increases. This aspirational American theme echoes everywhere you turn. In his commencement speech to the graduating class of Syracuse University, in 2013, George Saunders, the writer and professor, told the departing young people to be mindful of cultivating their awareness of

> that luminous part of you that exists beyond personality,
> your soul if you will, [which] is as bright and shining as
> any that has ever been. Bright as Shakespeare's. Bright as
> Gandhi's. Bright as Mother Teresa's.[1]

Did Saunders know he was channeling Emerson ("All that Adam had, all that Caesar could, you have and can do. . . . Your dominion is as great as theirs. . . . Build, therefore, your own world")? Who knows. What is indisputable is that "cosmic optimism," as Emerson described it, beats at the heart of the American dream. He warned his countrymen to remember their spiritual foundations since vaunting materialism and ambition decoupled from self-awareness lead only to degradation.

"It is the vulgarity of this country to believe that naked wealth, unrelieved by any use or design, is merit," he wrote (*WCS*). "Americans have many values but they have not Faith or Hope" (*MTR*). To resuscitate these dormant qualities, we must pay attention to the health and well-being of the spirit.

How Waldo Became Ralph Waldo Emerson

Ralph Waldo Emerson was born in Boston on May 25, 1803, the third of eight children in the family of the Reverend William Emerson, a seventh-generation Unitarian minister, and his wife, Ruth Haskins. At the age of thirty-three, William died suddenly of dysentery, leaving Ruth on her own to raise their children with few social prospects and little money. With the exception of his handicapped brother, Bulkeley, Ralph—who liked to be called Waldo—was the least promising of the Emerson boys. Moody, introverted, and sickly, he suffered through a difficult childhood haunted by feelings of unworthiness in the long shadow of his outgoing brothers. Lodged in his basement room, overlooking the local cemetery, he buried himself in books and daydreamed, struggled with morbid ruminations—only five of the eight Emerson children survived to adulthood—and worried for his family's safety.

Ruth opened a boardinghouse to make ends meet and was joined by her sister-in-law, Mary Moody Emerson, a brilliant, eccentric, pious spinster who became Waldo's most influential teacher. With the aid of a social charity, he entered Harvard at age sixteen and was the youngest pupil in the university's first class, although his academic record was mediocre (he graduated thirtieth in a class of fifty-nine). Drawn to philosophy and religion, Waldo chose to enter the family business and enrolled at Harvard Divinity School two years later with plans to become a minister. After completing his studies, he went to work as an itinerant preacher, and, during an engagement in New Hampshire, made the acquaintance of a lovely, sixteen-year-old poet named Ellen Tucker, with whom he fell deeply in love. The couple married two years later.

Already sick with tuberculosis, Ellen struggled with her health, a battle Waldo fought alongside her for the next eighteen months, determined to save her life. Waldo later described this period as "the happiest and most miserable of his life,"[2] ending with Ellen's death at age nineteen, and Waldo falling into a suicidal depression. Eight months after losing his beloved, unable to shake his awful despair, Waldo made a fateful decision that took him to Ellen's tomb at Mount Auburn Cemetery on the morning of March 29, 1832 (an episode we'll look at later on). This transformational experience helped to shock him back to life and set Waldo on his life course. He resigned his prestigious position at Boston's Second Church, having lost his traditional Christian faith, and set sail for Europe a few months later, determined to salvage his gifts and embark on his life as a professional writer. His neighbor John Stuart Mill provided him with letters of introduction that opened the drawing rooms of several famous writers, including William Wordsworth, who underwhelmed him, Samuel Taylor Coleridge, whom he found stodgy and uninspiring, and Thomas Carlyle, who became a lifelong friend.

After three months in Europe, Waldo returned to Boston and reinvented himself as a lecturer on the Lyceum circuit. The Lyceum movement was part lecture bureau, part debating society, a new venture in popular education catering to people who wished to shed outdated ways of thinking and open their minds to new ideas (in other words, seekers). Though Waldo's performance style was less than scintillating (a neighbor reportedly likened his onstage presence to that of an upright coffin), his message was electrifying and offered up in his rich baritone voice. It wasn't long before his appearances were selling out, setting Waldo on the professional path that would support his family for the next half century, traveling up and down the eastern seaboard by railroad and as far west as the Utah Territories.

Four years after Ellen's death, Waldo married a devout woman named Lydia (Lidian) Jackson, and the couple welcomed two sons and two daughters into their family over the next eight years. The Emersons settled into a large, two-story house on Concord Turnpike where Waldo, heartened by the warm public reaction to his lectures, threw himself into completing his first collection of essays adapted from his public talks. In 1841, he published *Nature* and sold out the first printing in less than a month. Suddenly, Waldo was catapulted from the ranks of traveling speaker and disgraced ex-minister into Ralph Waldo Emerson, the George Washington of American letters, the Oracle of Concord, and the spiritual voice of his generation. He was a mentor and friend to a generation of writers and thinkers whose work would come to define the nineteenth-century American character. Besides Henry David Thoreau, his Concord circle included Walt Whitman, Nathaniel Hawthorne, Herman Melville, Margaret

Fuller, Bronson Alcott, and William Ellery Channing. Whitman credited Waldo's early praise for his first book, *Leaves of Grass*, with rescuing the ambitious poet from a fledgling's morass of self-doubt. "I was simmering, simmering, simmering, Emerson brought me to a boil," Whitman confided.[3]

Thoreau took a job as a handyman, gardener, and tutor to the Emerson children in 1842. His friendship with Waldo was complicated, filled with mutual admiration, head butting, and exasperation along with genuine reverence. Waldo admired Henry's preternatural connection to the local biosphere and his encyclopedic knowledge of its inhabitants, while Henry, who was Waldo's junior by seven years, grew enamored of his mentor's spiritual presence and self-reliant philosophy. One year after meeting Henry, Waldo's youngest son, Wallie, succumbed to scarlet fever, a loss Waldo counted the most tragic of his life. He poured his grief into the poem "Threnody," which is considered one of the greatest elegies in American literature. Waldo's lifelong pattern of coping with major loss through redoubled creativity sustained him and suited his philosophy of self-regeneration.

An avid reader of contemplative books, from Seneca's *Letters from a Stoic* to the bawdy essays of his favorite, Michel de Montaigne, Waldo was drawn to literature aimed at opening the spiritual eye, elucidating existential questions, and awakening readers to their innate wisdom. He was such a fan of the Bhagavad Gita that Waldo was known around Concord as the "Yankee Hindoo." His mission "to bring light to the darkened lives of men" never wavered. In today's marketplace, we categorize such books as self-help, but the idea of sequestering wisdom literature away from the rest of general interest would have struck Waldo as absurd. Montaigne's biographer, Sarah Bakewell, says as much of her own subject, writing that "the distinction between self-help and academic philosophy wouldn't have made much sense" to the sixteenth-century French nobleman.[4] Waldo insisted that philosophy not aimed at helping us deal with everyday matters did not deserve its name. Like Montaigne and the Stoics before him, he believed that philosophy's sole purpose is to help us live better, more self-aware lives and appreciate our astounding existence.

Waldo was an avid abolitionist who pressured Abraham Lincoln to fight harder to end slavery and helped to influence the political efforts of several prominent Afro-Americans of his day and after. When social reformer and statesman Frederick Douglass heard him speak, he was profoundly moved by Waldo's description of what it means to be an "anti-slave"—a topic we'll look at later on. And when sociologist W. E. B. Du Bois learned of Waldo's ideas about "double consciousness"—the split between one's private and public self—it had an undeniable impact on his teachings about emancipation.[5] Waldo's greatest social influence came as the leader of the Transcendentalist movement, which cropped up in the 1840s. Heavily influenced by Eastern spirituality, Transcendentalism was an outcry against the pious religiosity of the day; it reflected a widespread dissatisfaction with the bloodlessness and rationalism of the mainstream Protestant church. Transcendentalists longed to have more intense, direct spiritual experience, and Waldo—who had come to view Jesus as an enlightened human being like the Buddha, Socrates, or Lao Tse, rather than as the only son of God—was their natural leader. "The noxious exaggeration [of] the person of Jesus" (*DSA*) had turned the historical Christ into a demi-god, subverting the universality of Jesus's teaching and replacing it with idolatry, he believed. Transcendentalism reversed this dogma, returned spiritual life to its rightful place as an outgrowth of our inherent divinity.

Over the next four decades, he maintained an ambitious speaking schedule that began to slow down only in the late 1860s, when Waldo's increasing forgetfulness, likely the early signs of Alzheimer's disease, made it impossible for him to continue. In 1871, he embarked on a final lecture tour of the Midwest before finally retiring from public life. According to his daughter Edith, the slow fading of his memory ceased to trouble Waldo as time went on. "Father is very well and very happy," she wrote in a letter to Carlyle. "Mother often says that he is the happiest person she ever knew—he is so uniformly in good spirits and waking each morning in a joyful mood."[6]

On April 19, 1882, Waldo became ill with pneumonia after being caught in a thunderstorm during his daily walk. Six days later, he was dead. On his last day, he dressed himself despite his wife's protests and spent the day as usual, reading and writing in his ground floor study. According to Edith, he finally agreed to retire early but refused all attempts to assist him in closing up his study for the night. With the family looking on, Waldo slowly walked from window to window, pulling the shutters and locking them. Then he took the fire apart in the hearth, as was his custom, setting the sticks on end, one by one, and separating out the burning coals. After Waldo had completed his duties, he took up his reading lamp and climbed the stairs to his room, leaving his study for the last time.

What Is Self-Reliance?

The principles of Waldo's philosophy are universal and require no spiritual faith to put into practice.

- Each person creates her own reality.

- Nothing (save physical violence) can harm you except with your permission.

- Obstacles can become opportunities.

- Virtue is the portal to happiness.

- The God in you connects you to the God in all things.

- Character is destiny.

- There is no me without you (interdependence is everything).

- Mortality is the greatest teacher.

- Wonder and awe are the keys to the kingdom.

- Life without self-knowledge is not worth living.

Self-reliance has nothing to do with selfishness. This is the single greatest misconception surrounding Waldo's central teaching, which has been associated too often with toxic individualism and Ayn Randian phallocracy. Waldo makes it eminently clear that self-reliance is first and foremost a spiritual practice. "Self-reliance is reliance on God," he said (*FSL*). "There is nothing so weak as an egotist" (*TYA*). In his teaching, you will see how he factors in the physical with the metaphysical, the material with the transcendent, and encourages us to dissolve the false duality between spirituality and everyday life.

We have never needed this integration more. "Alas for America . . . the air is loaded with poppy, with imbecility, with dispersions and sloth," Waldo lamented in 1840,[7] when the population of Boston was ninety thousand and the opiate epidemic was not yet imagined. He deplored the passivity of his contemporaries—"Timorous, desponding whimperers, afraid of truth and each other" (*SR*)—and warned that greed and loneliness would become chronic American malaises if we abandoned our spiritual values. "My own quarrel with America [is that] the geography is sublime, the men are not," he admitted (*CBW*). Waldo's prescience on the state of the American soul has been borne out in tragic proportions. Depression, anxiety, addiction, and fear levels are on a catastrophic rise. Between 2007 and 2018, the suicide rates of young people aged ten to twenty-four increased nearly 60 percent.[8] Rates of deliberate self-harm among ten- to fourteen-year-old girls, by cutting or self-poisoning, nearly tripled in the US between 2009 and 2015.[9] From superbugs to fire tornados, poisonous waters to fishless seas, we're inundated with warnings of present and future destruction around the clock. COVID-19 multiplied this terror, turning the planet into an earth-size petri dish for propagating global panic. A sizable poll that aimed at measuring Americans' various fears reported that more than 70 percent live in dread of natural disasters, and comparable statistics apply to cyber terrorism, government corruption, civil war, random violence, and ending up homeless in the streets.[10]

Waldo's teachings help to dispel the illusion of our own powerlessness, turning the reader's wisdom eye toward spiritual awakening. Along with the Stoics, he reminds us that this expanded perspective is available to all who take the time to grapple with their experience, investigate their point of view, and separate truth from falsehood. This is what constitutes an examined life. "The one thing [Emerson] is adamant about is that we should look—we must look—for that is the liquor of life, that brooding upon issues, that attention to thought even as we weed the garden or milk the cow," poet Mary Oliver writes.[11] In the light of self-awareness, the conventional world reveals its true nature as a stand-in for a deeper reality. Think of those one-dimensional folly houses you drive by in the English countryside, their unreality concealed by a showy façade. Waldo believed that our attachment to appearances and surface illusions prevents us from recognizing our true home in the universe.

Self-reliance drew from three philosophical streams, starting with Waldo's ingrained Christianity. Jesus's teachings remained dear to him despite his apostasy from the church. This disconnect is mirrored in the movement of many Christians away from tradition in favor of updated approaches to faith today. The number of Christians who remain loyal to the old-time church has dropped by nearly half since the turn of the millennium.[12] As indelibly as it was woven into Waldo's character, Christianity pervades American culture to a degree we sometimes forget.* Christians who find themselves struggling with ecclesiastical doubt while maintaining their devotion to the teachings of Jesus will recognize in Waldo's conflict their own disaffection and ambivalence.

Beyond its Christian influences, self-reliance is the philosophical love child of two apparently star-crossed forebears, Transcendentalism and Stoicism. These divergent schools of thought have more in common with one another than you might think. Transcendentalism was a spiritual rebellion against the hierarchical, sexist, nature-negative, sin-and-redemption-focused doctrines of the Protestant church. Transcendentalists sought a more direct relationship with God than was offered through stodgy church rituals; they sought a faith strengthened by intuition, emotion, revelation, and our natural connection to "the inviolable order of the world." Focused on the potential of human goodness, Transcendentalism teaches that spiritual intermediaries are unnecessary for maintaining a close connection with God.

Though the Transcendentalist movement was short-lived, lasting only twenty years or so, the roots of this philosophy run deep in a nation where originality and personal freedom are so highly prized. Waldo's notion of an "original relationship to the universe" (N), and his belief that a divine spirit pervades all of nature

---

* There has never been a non-Christian president of the United States. The Moral Majority continues to preside over the conservative wing of American politics. "In God We Trust," meaning the God of the Bible, appears on the dollar bill, and, in 2021, the Supreme Court added another evangelical judge to its ranks, threatening the survival of anti-Christian rights, including abortion, contraception, and same-sex marriage. This is a *Christian* country to its roots.

(including human nature), became inseparable from transcendental American ideas of self-determination, individual rights, and spiritual liberty. When Lady Gaga belts her anthem "Born This Way" to stadiums of freak flag–flying devotees, she's paying homage to this current of emancipation. Many of this country's most heated debates, particularly those concerning racial justice, gender equality, religious liberties, and the sacrilegious abuse of Mother Nature, emerge from the transcendentalist playbook as well.

Optimism is another legacy of Transcendentalism, but this wasn't a hopefulness based on denying the evil of which people are capable. Instead, Waldo's "cosmic optimism" faces the brutal facts of human fallibility without losing sight of their redemptive potential. When Dr. Martin Luther King Jr., an ardent Transcendentalist, preached that "the arc of the moral universe is long but it bends toward justice," he was echoing such cosmic optimism. Waldo insisted that even in the worst of circumstances, goodness and wisdom are possible. "This time, like all times, is a very good one, if we but know what to do with it," he wrote (*TAS*). Though gimlet-eyed about humanity's failings, he was hopeful when it came to individual people and our ability to better our lives.

This faith in self-improvement is integral to Stoicism as well. This pragmatic, down-to-earth philosophy, popularized two thousand years ago in Greece and Rome, was forged in the tragedies of the ancient world. Emperor Marcus Aurelius wrote his *Meditations* as the Antonine Plague swept through his realm, killing a third of its citizenry. Stoicism is at its best

when circumstances are at their worst, which explains its growing popularity today. The Stoics put forth practical tools for
thriving in the face of challenge, including the sort of "spiritual
exercises" you will find at the end of this book; in fact, marked
parallels have been identified between Stoic spiritual exercises
and cognitive behavioral therapy.[13] Their insistence on self-
investigation, gratitude for what we have, humility toward what
we don't know (and can't control), the benefits of adversity, the
freedom to change perspective, and the Divine Mystery that infuses the world coincide precisely with Waldo's teachings. The
Stoic practice of accepting life as it is (*amor fati*), even when
times are difficult, and their focus on the growth potential of
remembering our mortality (*memento mori*) are integral to self-
reliance as well. Finally, Waldo and the Stoics shared a central
philosophical question: namely, how can we cultivate happiness
(*eudaimonia*) in a fragile, unpredictable, dangerous world? They
agreed that authentic well-being is only possible through "rational transcendence," by taking refuge in "the last of the human
freedoms" (in the words of psychologist Viktor Frankl): the
ability to choose our attitude in any given set of circumstances.
This freedom allows us to remain *ourselves* when life robs us of
the things we cherish.

How to Use This Book

These twelve lessons mirror the perennial steps on the path of
personal awakening. We begin with originality and character,

the discovery of an interior world, and how to use self-inquiry as a doorway to wisdom. In Lesson Two, we move to the question of perspective, Waldo's insights into the nature of self-created reality, and how shifting your angle of vision can radically improve your quality of life. Next, we explore the ways in which nonconformity contributes to the process of self-realization. In Lesson Four, we turn to paradox and contradiction, and Waldo's insistence (shared with the Stoics) that a person's flaws and limitations hold intrinsic value on the path of personal excellence. We explore the link between confidence and resilience in Lesson Five, and why self-esteem magnetizes opportunities and like-minded souls to a person, as if alerting the universe to her intentions. Next, we consider the vitality that stems from connecting to the natural world and how plugging into this spiritual source energizes us, revealing the One Mind, or Over-Soul, at play in everything we do.

In Lesson Seven, we unpack Waldo's insights into fear and courage, and we look at how self-reliance neutralizes dread and anxiety by emphasizing the power of personal choice. Love and intimacy arise from conscious choice, too, as we learn in Lesson Eight; here, we consider the underestimated value of friendship, those conflicts likely to trouble the lover's heart, and the transpersonal dimension of love itself. Warmheartedness is also helpful when confronting adversity, which, in turn, initiates one into maturity and wholeness, as you'll see in Lesson Nine. Gratitude is a spiritual practice that leads to resilience as well, including the realization that destruction often leads to renewal. The capacity to prevail over obstacles also spurs optimism, as we discover in

Lesson Ten; acknowledging how little we actually control elicits a particular sort of faith, in fact. Such faith is palpable, experiential, and predicated on reverence and awe. In Lesson Eleven, we explore Waldo's splendid teachings on astonishment and beauty as portals to self-knowledge, and we consider why an awareness of the miraculous in everyday existence is crucial to our well-being. Finally, in Lesson Twelve, we examine the promise of enlightenment, the transformation of consciousness that becomes possible by taking the "erect position" in our life, remaining mindful of the present moment, and freeing ourselves from the oppressive constructs of the self-absorbed, crepuscular mind.

These core teachings are presented through the lens of a passionate seeker, not as a scholarly enterprise. They offer practical wisdom for real-life people who want to live happier, more imaginative, and more passionate lives. My style is prescriptive, not theoretical, colloquial rather than academic. I focus on Waldo the man, not the gray eminence, on the brilliant-but-flawed outlier he truly was, irascible, complex, entrenched in his times, and painfully aware of his own failings. Waldo's cultural training as a nineteenth-century male Boston Brahmin led to his harboring some antiquated notions concerning sex, women, race, and social mores, but these shortcomings, while unfortunate, did not impact his spiritual teachings in any appreciable way. Like most authors of his period, he defaulted to masculine pronouns in his writing, and I've done my best to balance this grammatical bias by introducing *she* and *her* whenever possible. Readers familiar with Emerson's work may be struck by the conspicuous absence of his poetry (my least favorite part of his oeuvre) here; also, many of the topics he wrote about (history, economics, cosmology, art theory) are nowhere to be found, having little bearing on the subject at hand.

These twelve lessons are intended as a road map for authentic living, a user's guide to Emerson's forgotten wisdom as it applies to the problems we face today. If you use them well, and put them into practice, they have the power to change your life.

On Originality

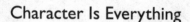

Character Is Everything

"A man's fortune is his character."

Becoming Yourself

Waldo was a lackluster, socially awkward child of whom little was expected in a family of confident overachievers, as I've said. Passive, dreamy, and prone to mood swings, he saw himself as an "unfocused laggard" and despaired of ever amounting to much. He was "always listening," according to biographer Van Wyck Brooks, and was

> an obscure little boy, chubby, awkward, affectionate as a puppy, with a sluggish mind, a mind heavy and overcast like a summer of charged electricity . . . a shrinking, retreating little creature, but full of wonder.[1]

Waldo loved his books, worshipped his brothers, and had dreams of greatness but was also tormented by doubt and self-judgment. His composure around others masked a passionate temperament, extreme emotions, and a fair amount of social anxiety.

"I ramble among doubts to which my reason offers no solution," he wrote in a letter to his aunt Mary.[2] A Dickensian figure notorious for her brilliance and oddities, unmarried Mary Moody Emerson was Waldo's first mentor and influencer, the personification of originality in the eyes of her timid nephew. At four-feet-three-inches tall, Mary was a fiery Calvinist and autodidact, who read Cicero and Shakespeare for breakfast, wore a burial shroud when she traveled, and slept in a coffin-shaped bed, so eager was she to return to her Maker. Mary moved through the world with a prehensile energy that Waldo admired. "She had the misfortune of spinning with greater velocity than any of the other tops," he wrote,[3] though he deemed himself sluggish, distracted, and moody. Mary encouraged her introverted nephew to throw off his shell, test his limits, and set his sights on the highest goals. "Scorn trifles, lift your aims [and] do what you are afraid to do," she told him.[4]

Waldo learned that becoming oneself, striving for an original relation to the universe, is the purpose of a human life. He came to believe that character is everything, personally and spiritually, and that unless an individual knows herself, she cannot fulfill her unique purpose in life. This purpose transcends convention and utility. "It is not . . . the chief end of man that he should make a fortune and beget children whose end is likewise to make a fortune, but . . . that he should explore himself," he maintained

(*AOE*). Looking to others for approval is futile when it comes to developing personal character; instead, we must look to ourselves for guidance since there comes a "time in every man's education when he arrives at the conviction that envy is ignorance; that imitation is suicide" (*SR*). One's mandate is to bring what is *hers* into the world, and harvest the fruits of her natural being. This is only possible when she becomes deeply acquainted with herself *as she truly is*, outside the spotlight of public opinion.

Waldo viewed self-inquiry is an unsurpassed method for personal growth. The practice of exploring philosophical questions to open the mind, and gain insight into the nature of reality, dates back to a time long before the Stoics, when the sages of India first posed the question "Who am I?" as the starting point on the path of self-discovery. Socrates carried on this practice with the admonition to "Know thyself" as a doorway to the examined life. We create our perceived reality through the funhouse mirror of personal bias, which is why self-inquiry is necessary for self-reliance. It's impossible to "do your own thing" without first knowing who you are. This means doing the humbling work of examining parts of yourself you'd prefer to ignore in order to integrate them into your awareness.

Waldo learned from watching Aunt Mary that while this difficult woman could be off-putting, it was precisely Mary's willingness to be who she was, and allow her faults to be what they were, that brought such force and effectiveness to her character. Mary did not waste time in a struggle to conform, while her nephew was an insecure people pleaser. Fortunately, Waldo would outgrow much of his self-tormenting behavior and make peace with his peculiarities. He would come to see his debilities and defects as teachers, as inherent, necessary aspects of his character. Over time, he came to develop the ability to survey his inner landscape through the eyes of an objective witness, to view his shortcomings not with tragic regret but as the comic failures of a limited person.

You Are Interesting

Pop artist Andy Warhol made a parallel discovery after struggling with extreme self-loathing as a boy. Warhol, who hired me as an editor at his magazine when I arrived in New York, began life as an effeminate, pimply-faced, squeamish child in a family of Polish, working-class immigrants transplanted in Pittsburgh, Pennsylvania. At an early age, Warhol began experimenting with social personas, hoping to create a character congruent with the outlier-homosexual artist he sensed he might become someday. As Waldo had glimmers of future greatness as a boy, Warhol had a nascent awareness of his own originality from an early age. Yet it wasn't until he stepped off a Greyhound bus in New York City, in 1949, and discovered a downtown art scene filled with fellow misfits, that this originality could effloresce into his genius.

Encouraged by his radical cohort, Warhol began slaying the sacred cows that were blocking his progress in the world of fine art. He transformed his glaring limitations—unimpressive draftsmanship, poor social skills, even premature hair loss—into brand trademarks he set about flaunting without apology. His lifelong inability to imitate others, along with an innate force of character, helped Warhol in recasting his introversion into a signature, gnomic style, and developing the unique approach to artmaking—tracing photographs onto blank canvases, then painting between the lines like a child with a coloring book—that would bring him international success. He even reframed his baldness as a point of interest, covering his head with multi-colored fright wigs that were guaranteed to get him noticed. While his critics viewed these strategies as mere affectations, they were integral to Warhol's genius, in fact, converting flaws into strengths through imagination. Although he was only sporadically happy, suffering terribly from romantic loneliness, Warhol was nevertheless always *himself*, whether chatting with a head of state or filming tattooed hustlers in flagrante delicto. He could no more disguise his originality than Aunt Mary could conceal her singular brilliance.

Both of them lived by what Waldo described as the law of "compensation." All of us are walking contradictions made of mismatched parts and anomalies. It is only through adaptation and imagination that we're able to combine our wayward, disparate parts into a unified whole, Waldo teaches. "Every sweet has its sour; every evil its good" (*C*). Each strength gives rise to a corresponding weakness, and every loss offers some kind of benefit. Waldo compared this seesaw effect to the paradoxical gains of a blind man whose hearing grows marvelously acute, or a financier who loses everything only to recognize his enslavement to material things and appreciate the liberating power of spiritual pursuits. Compensation reminds us that foibles always come with a flip side, and flaws can be catalysts for positive change when we

have the patience and determination to find the pony in the pro-
verbial pile of shit.

To make the law of compensation work for you, it's necessary
to identify which insecurities, losses, weaknesses, and failings you
try hardest to conceal from the world, and to consider how these
debilities might be viewed differently. Failing to recognize the latent potential in your defects leads you only to avoid your limitations while attempting to imitate the virtues of others. Instead,
try imagining the positive dividends these shortfalls might afford
you if you stopped judging them. When you succeed in viewing
your foibles this way, you become fascinated by rather than contemptuous of those peculiarities that set you apart from others.
"If men would avoid that general language and general manner in
which they strive to hide all that is peculiar and would say only
what was uppermost in their minds, after their individual manner, every man would be interesting," Waldo explained.[5]

Instead, we often reject our originality for no other reason
than that it is *ours*. This reflexive aversion points to a fundamen-
tal distrust of the spiritual intelligence moving through us. We
tend to ignore the obvious fact that a power source infinitely
more creative than the individual mind is animating our personal lives. "The mind common to the universe is disclosed to
the individual through his own nature," Waldo maintained.[6]
"My own mind is the direct revelation I have from God." He
instructs us to watch for that gleam of light "which flashes
across [the] mind from within," and to trust these unique in-
tuitions "more than the lustre of the firmaments of bards and
sages" (*SR*).

This requires that we pay attention to our inner guidance,

trusting the originality within us instead of bowing to the majority. Acquiescence is the enemy of authenticity, he warned. Still, we're trained to go along with the crowd, not push envelopes, and resist disobedience in order to be team players and model citizens. Such "incapacitating education"

> aim[s] to sink what is individual or personal in us. The
> book, the college, the school of art, the institution of any
> kind, stop with some past utterance of genius. They pin
> me down, they look backward, not forward. (*TAS*)

Systems theorist Buckminster Fuller, whose great-aunt Margaret Fuller was Waldo's platonic paramour, observed, "Everyone is born a genius but the process of living de-geniuses them."[7] Such de-geniusing begins in the classrooms of youth where deference and self-shrinking are enforced and encouraged. To remember that you are interesting, you must resist the siren call of imitation. Rather than queue up on the road most traveled, go where no path exists and leave a trail for others instead.

Follow the Bliss

Increasing your awareness of the voice inside you allows you to trust your own predilections. "None of us ever will accomplish anything excellent or commanding except when he listens to the whisper which is heard by him alone."[8] Waldo's emphasis on intuition over tuition, on adhesion to our inborn knowledge more than erudition picked up in books, is integral to self-reliance.

"Intuitive graspings" open your mind to messages from its higher intelligence.

> That which each man can do best none but his Maker
> can teach him. Our spontaneous action is always the best.
> You cannot, with your best deliberations and heed, come
> so close to any question as your spontaneous glance shall
> bring you. (*INT*)

Spontaneous action circumvents the self-doubting mind; when we trust this inner dictation, we prosper.

Studies of intuition support Waldo's teaching. Intuition is defined as the ability to know something without analytic reasoning and bridges the gap between the conscious and unconscious parts of the mind. Efficacy and authenticity are deeply linked to intuition as well. Satu Teerikangas, a Finnish researcher who specializes in the dynamics of strategic change, points out that intuition is prompted when "we travel from known to unknown cognitive terrain." By rejecting secondhand ideas and assumptions, we bring about a cognitive shift that "forces . . . everyday habitual masks down, inviting the authentic self to emerge," Teerikangas explains.[9] This assertion echoes Waldo's view of personal genius, the originality that is your natural birthright. "To believe your own thought, to believe that what is true for you in your private heart is true for all men, that is genius," he tells us (*SR*). Faithful listening to "the still small voice within" enlarges and defines your creative power. "It seems to be true that the more exclusively idiosyncratic a man is, the more infinite," Waldo noted.[10]

Females have a distinct advantage over boys and men, apparently, when it comes to intuition. The female corpus collosum—white matter that links the brain's right and left hemispheres—is thicker than its male counterpart's. This advantage allows women and girls to access both cerebral hemispheres with greater facility; they're able to integrate emotions and gut feelings into rational decision-making with greater ease. ("I, as always, venerate the oracular nature of woman," Emerson wrote in his journal.[11]) Males tend to be more compartmentalized in their thinking and less flexible in moving from logic to intuition and more integrated forms of knowledge.[12]

Judith Orloff, a psychologist who specializes in treating empaths and sensitive people, deems intuition the female superpower, citing the case of a woman she worked with who discovered her suppressed intuition in the nick of time. Faced with a hard professional decision, this female CEO was having a difficult time "thinking the problem through" to a logical solution. Rather than force this momentous decision, she was advised by Orloff to ask herself in a quiet moment, "Is this the best deal for me to get involved with?" This turn inward relaxed her cogitating, logic-seeking mind and gave this high-octane overachiever the answer for which she'd been waiting. Orloff describes how this patient "saw a flash of the *Titanic* sinking," which told the CEO all she needed to know about which option to take. "Using this image and her gut feeling led her to opt out. That business turned out to be a failure."[13]

When Mary Moody Emerson was asked how she managed to walk her own path in a society in which women were second-class citizens, she replied, "I danced the music of my own imajanation

[sic]."[14] In an interview about his own creative process, Andy Warhol confided, "When I have to think about it, I know the picture is wrong. . . . The more you have to decide [and choose], the more wrong it gets."[15] Waldo was adamant in his belief that "we know better than we do" and that genius is more reliable than ratiocination.

> We need only obey . . . and by lowly listening, we shall hear
> the right word. . . . Into us flows the stream evermore of
> thought from we know not whence. We do not determine
> what we think; we only open our senses, clear away as
> we can all obstruction from the facts, and let God think
> through us. (SL)

Following this divine inclination leads a person to her bliss. The exhausting struggle to *make things happen* is also alleviated, as Waldo learned after years of self-doubt. "Can you believe, Waldo Emerson, that you may relieve yourself of this perpetual perplexity of choosing, & by putting your ear close to the soul, learn always the true way," he marveled in his journal.[16] Such listening arouses our primordial intelligence, and its messages are often a revelation.

On Wilderness

Waldo would have been scornful of the over-domestication of contemporary life. Obsessed with convenience and time-saving, we've enshrined an ideal of affluence that denudes our existence of wildness. It's no surprise that many are suffocating from an excess of synthetic, prefabricated, unnatural experience stripped of authentic flavor. "The problem of man's existence, is unique in the whole of nature," wrote psychologist Erich Fromm.[17] "He has fallen out of nature, as it were, and is still in it; he is partly divine, partly animal; partly infinite, partly finite."[18]

We're not meant to divorce ourselves from the grit and challenge of terrestrial life, Waldo reminds us. In our technologically advanced era, there's a growing desire for more raw, unvarnished, *simple* experience to revitalize our slick, overcivilized existence. Consumers look to wilderness companies such as Outward Bound for the opportunity to commune with nature, red in tooth and claw. These establishments provide a useful service, to be sure, while also preying on the public's spiritual hunger, charging whopping sums of money for customers to be dropped in the middle of nowhere with nothing but a backpack and a thermos of brew. The pervasive human longing to tame nature (if not to transcend her demands completely) compromises character, Waldo warned, and breeds derivative, bloodless, secondhand people, pale imitations of their rough-hewn relations. "A sturdy lad from New Hampshire is worth a hundred of these city dolls," he claimed (*SR*), contrasting the wherewithal of country children with the cosseted upbringing of urban kids.

Whether we accept this simplistic dichotomy or not, Waldo is making an important point. When we allow the animal self to go soft and ignore the call of the wild, we sacrifice an essential part of what it means to be human. That is why it's crucial to find ways to *undomesticate* ourselves by regaining a measure of wildness in our lives. Whether we do so through cooking outdoors, forest bathing, going on retreat, or simply disconnecting our devices one day a week to remember how it feels not to be attached to machines, such deprogramming is critical to our mental and spiritual health. We should examine what we've relinquished for the sake of efficiency and comfort, and how we can regain all that we've lost to the culture of convenience.

Waldo teaches that our "aboriginal" guidance is inseparable from nature, emerging from a source we do not control. Nature is our greatest teacher, he insists, providing wisdom lessons that cannot be accessed elsewhere (an insight we will explore later on). Waldo cemented his reputation for blasphemy by placing the gospel of nature above that of the Bible, in fact, encouraging us to become devotees of the wild. Aligning ourselves to the rhythms of nature, we're viscerally yoked to the present moment, stilling the mind and refining our awareness. Time spent outside the human-made world provides similar effects to those of meditation; both offer naked immersion in the present moment and the exposure of bare-bones consciousness to the natural light of unfiltered attention. They're an opportunity to reinhabit our bodies and to explore our interior wilderness and the immediacy of our lived experience.

Here's an experiment you might like to try. Find a quiet spot away from people, and set a timer for five minutes. Now, close your eyes, rest your hands in your lap, and bring your attention to the current of energy circulating through your limbs, torso, hands, and feet, behind your eyes, in your gut, and up to the crown of your head. Notice the sensations arising in your body *as sensations* without assigning them mental labels, and note how this nonverbal awareness sharpens your felt experience of being in the body. Take note, too, of how this in-seeing permits you to drop into the zone of silence below the nonstop monologue of your cogitating brain. When the timer goes off, open your eyes and pay attention to how your embodied experience has changed. Try writing about any thoughts or feelings that arose in you during this time-out. Connecting to your natural being in this way has surprising mental, physical, and spiritual benefits.[19] The body and mind are energized in this tranquil state; stress drops away and leaves you refreshed.

Exposure to the wild liberates us from our human-made troubles, instilling a lost sense of innocence—or gladness—knowing we are still in the Garden. "In the presence of Nature, a wild delight runs through the man in spite of real sorrows," Waldo explained. "Nature says, —he is my creature, and [in spite of] all his impertinent griefs, he shall be glad with me" (*N*). Wilderness dwarfs our human woes against the backdrop of eternity, reminding us of our secret garden, the untouched space within that is ours alone. In "A Secret Life," poet Stephen Dunn compares this out-of-bounds realm to the interior space you would want "most protected if the government said you can protect one thing, all else is ours."[20] This interior wilderness is unassailably private and resistant to domestication. Immersing yourself in nature keeps it alive. Waldo learned this as a young man, when a long walk in the woods around Boston was the only medicine powerful enough to ease his alienation. Saint Augustine coined the phrase *solvitur ambulando* to describe why wandering brings solace to the turbulent mind; hiking along these wilderness trails, Waldo was able to drop his intellectual armor, hear the sermon of the trees, and tap into the source-root of his genius.

He makes it clear that in order to access the wild, we must cultivate the art of being alone. When solitude is denied to us, we lose contact with our inner world.

> At times the whole world seems to be in a conspiracy to importune you with trifles. . . . Friend, client, child, sickness, fear, want, charity, all knock at once at thy closet door and say,—"Come out unto us." But keep thy state; come not into their confusion. The power men possess to annoy me I give them by a weak curiosity. (SR)

Yet we abdicate our aloneness on a regular basis, preferring distraction to solitude. We're pulled between opposing forces, the biological pull toward attachment, affiliation, cooperation, and social connection, and the solitude necessary for attunement to the whisper only you can hear. With practice, solitude becomes the "place where we are least alone," in Lord Byron's words.[21] The imagination is stimulated by empty space and play-alone time; solitary interludes are good for strengthening character and acceding to *metamorphosis* (a word Waldo preferred to *transformation*). Solitude is especially important for young people who need time on their own to ponder, muddle through, and imagine the life before them. Research reveals that teenagers who can't tolerate being alone fail to develop their creative talent more than those who enjoy their own company, since the muse requires solitary activities to develop her talents.[22]

Studies also show that online connectivity is making young people less tolerant of solitude as well as demonstrably less empathetic.[23] Given the choice to do nothing for fifteen minutes or deliver themselves a mild electroshock, nearly half of the young subjects in one experiment chose the pain over idleness.[24] Solitude also increases our capacity for intimacy, paradoxically, by teaching a person to tolerate the space between herself and the other. As psychologist D. W. Winnicott put it, "The person who has developed the capacity to be alone is never alone."[25] This confirms the connection between solitude and self-reliance; also, between wildness and insight. Insight requires self-confrontation, which always includes a thorough acquaintance with our own shadow.

Gifts of the Shadow

The shadow is that off-limits part of the psyche where we conceal aspects of ourself that threaten love and approval from others and increase the likelihood that our group will reject us. The psychological shadow contains not only guilt, shame, fear, and so on, but also—frequently—aspects of originality and personal genius, those nonconforming traits that make us unique.

Waldo was painfully aware of the courage it takes to navigate our hidden parts. He also knew that until one faces the qualities she finds most threatening and confusing in herself, she can never become self-reliant. Once again, we are masses of contradictions; to be human is to be hyphenate. On any given day, the average human being is weak-strong, generous-stingy, ambitious-exhausted, affectionate-reprehensible, courageous-afraid. She denies her rich complexity by avoiding the contents of her shadow, robbing her life of depth and perspective. A shadowless painting is shallow and incomplete; human character without its darker dimension is also drained of power and profundity.

For example, I know of a struggling artist who seemed unable to uncover her own originality. Her paintings were competent, well-executed, and forgettable, lacking authenticity and edge. This personable, well-adjusted, kindhearted individual was having a terrible time understanding what was missing. One day during a studio class, her teacher came by to critique her canvas, cocked her head, and suggested—out of the blue—that the fledgling painter experiment with using more black in her work. This comment confused her but she decided to give it a try. No sooner had her first brushstroke of black hit the canvas than her work began to improve. The paintings became bolder, more defined, more unique, more challenging, and far more evocative. Black became a signature of her work, and this increased daring at the easel prompted questions for her as a human being. How had she played it too safe in her life? Why was she such a people pleaser? Why had she constructed such a sunny persona and hidden her darker elements, her conflicts, anger, hunger . . . the parts that didn't make sense? Tapping into her shadow on canvas encouraged this artist to do more of this in her life. Over time, this led to an overall deepening of feeling, a greater commitment to authenticity, and the surprising realization that what she'd kept hidden, cloaked in the shadows of fear and shame, was also the source of her creative power.

A hundred years before Carl Jung popularized the psychological shadow, Waldo warned against excessive self-sanitizing. Guarded as a person might be in public, she must be able to drop her defenses and delusions when she is alone. Otherwise, she remains a stranger to herself and the truth of her own character. "We can no more half things and get [the good] than we can get a light without shadow," Waldo wrote. "Drive out nature with a fork, she comes running back" (*C*). The contents of the shadow are unpredictable, however, and pose a serious threat to the status quo, which is why societies encourage citizens to keep their extremes to themselves and repress what is wild and unique. Too much freedom and truthfulness makes it harder for the society to manipulate people; excessive originality poses a clear and present danger to structures of power that seek to control us. Unfortunately, what's good for the group often spells disaster for the individual who aspires to self-expression, since suppressing the shadow interferes with flourishing. We lose access to those hidden parts of ourselves that thrive on standing apart, and the wellness that comes from feeling whole and integrated. As Jung observed, "You do not become enlightened by imagining figures of light, but by making the darkness conscious."[26] Waldo agreed wholeheartedly.

To know your shadow parts better, you can begin by asking yourself a series of key questions: Which aspects of your character do you conceal in the shadow? Which aptitudes, appetites, gifts, and powers do you keep hidden in order to belong to the group and earn others' acceptance? Do you "shrink to fit" into environments where you need to stay small to survive? How would your life benefit from restoring these disowned parts and incorporating them into your character? Waldo wants us to open the cellar door and look carefully at what we've buried; to hide from nothing, investigate the darkness, and make use of what the shadow has to teach us.

Integration leads to self-trust. The more you're able to accept your checkered character, the more unreservedly you can join the human race; by dropping the wall of self-avoidance, you no longer feel quite so separate from others. Removing the obstacles to your authenticity, illuminating your shadow parts, you discern that you have a natural path. Waldo wrote that a person

> is like a ship in a river; he runs against obstructions on
> every side but one, on that side all obstruction is taken
> away and he sweeps serenely over a deepening channel into
> an infinite sea. (*SL*)

Each of us has a "selecting principle" that draws what is genuinely ours toward us. In the words of theologian Howard Thurman, "What is mine will know my face."[27] By virtue of this "inevitable nature," Waldo wrote, "private will is overpowered. . . . [In spite of] our efforts or our imperfections, your genius will speak from you and mine from me. That which we are, we shall teach, not voluntarily but involuntarily" (*O*). Thus, we open ourselves to our natural bounty. "Thoughts come into our minds by avenues which we never left open, and thoughts go out of our minds through avenues which we never voluntarily opened" (*O*). We see the truth that our individual mind is inseparable from the one Mind of God, that mysterious effulgence refracted through the lens of personal perspective. This point of view is what makes us unique. How we see is who we are and what we have to offer the world.

⊰ THE BRIEF ⊱

Self-knowledge is the first step toward self-reliance. Increasing awareness of your true nature, attuning to your inner guidance, you accelerate the process of becoming yourself. Listening to the whisper only you can hear, you discover that you are interesting, that your contradictions give you depth. Peculiarities, affinities, quirks, and losses make for character growth and originality. The more comfortable you are with being unique, the more capable you are of following your bliss. You're drawn to the wilderness of your being—the natural, undomesticated, God-given dimension, where you find sustenance, inspiration, and refuge. This wild part also contains your shadow, the psychological holding cell where you hide your shame, wounding, and fears, as well as your inherent gifts. You cannot be whole without your shadow. For self-realization to be possible, you must reclaim what you have buried.

LESSON TWO

On Perspective

You Are How You See

"People do not seem to realize that
their opinion of the world is also a
confession of their character."

The Laboratory of Experience

In the spring of 1825, a month after registering for Harvard
Divinity School, Waldo was afflicted with a blinding eye disease
likely linked to tuberculosis. He was forced to drop his studies,
cease reading and writing for several months, and undergo two
operations for cataracts. This sudden loss of his sight appears
to have had an awakening effect on the twenty-two-year-old
minister-to-be, however. Unable to bury himself in his books,
Waldo was forced to be alone with himself in a way that was

uncomfortable and new to him. In the solitude of his semi-blindness, he confronted aspects of himself that were hard to face—jealousy, depression, disempowerment, anger, and the specter of bisexuality—which he had subdued with cerebral pursuits. This forced convalescence at twenty-two became an initiation in self-reflection and extreme vulnerability.

Deprived of his vision, Waldo gained a deeper awareness of how susceptible a person's perspective is to shifting conditions and experiences. He realized that our angle of vision is always changing, like swapping filters on a camera lens, and that life is an experiment, first and foremost, taking place in the laboratory of the senses. We paint reality with our subjective colors and tint our perceptions with biases, judgments, fears, and desires unique to our given situation. We're not mere spectators trapped inside the kaleidoscopes of our minds, but are the cinematographers of our own life-movies, adjusting the cameras through which we see. Though we have little control over *what* we perceive, we have considerable influence over *how* we view things. "We do not determine what we think. We only open our senses, clear away as we can all obstruction from the facts, and let God think through us," Waldo wrote (*INT*). This enables us to become more discerning, separating impressions and interpretations from events themselves. As he explained,

> Life is a train of moods like strings of beads and as we pass through them, they prove to be many-colored lenses which paint the world their own hue and each shows only what lies in its focus. (*E*)

The subjective eye is fickle and untrustworthy, in other words, and its distortions must be scrutinized.

This hallucinatory component is especially tricky when it comes to how we see ourselves. Nowhere are we more delusional than in the domain of self-appraisal. When we become familiar with our own mood-trains, and how we color our experience, we come to realize how these polychrome filters alter our self-image, highlighting some traits, obscuring others. We perceive how our blind spots interfere with self-knowledge and increase the sense of separation from our surroundings. "There is an optical illusion about every person we meet," as Waldo put it.[1] This dysmorphia can be helped by a process known as *recentering* or *reperceiving*, which expands our point of view to include—but not be limited by—our own perspective. This teaches us to view our thoughts, emotions, and reactions as transitory patterns of mental activity instead of mistaking them for accurate representations of reality. "People only see what they are prepared to see," Waldo noted. Expectations expand or limit perception since "the health of the eye seems to demand a horizon" (*N*).

Knowing the limits of your own horizon allows you to extend it. A student of mine, a formidable, intelligent, highly successful professional in her early fifties, has a mortal fear of losing control, for example. When plans fluctuate or people change their minds, she goes to pieces, as if her world had become a chaotic jungle and she the unwitting prey. This otherwise confident individual seems to lose her bearings (indeed, herself) in the face of uncertainty. Aware though she is that such overreactions stem from memories of childhood abandonment, this rational knowledge is of little use since emotions, as everyone knows, are largely immune to reason (a conundrum we'll explore later). In my student's case, talk therapy hasn't helped much; instead, she's learned to relieve her anxiety by expressing her thoughts and feelings on paper. Self-reflection in the midst of her "breakdowns" helps her to regain some composure. Slowly, she is learning to shift *how* she sees, to question her paranoid narratives, and to change her knee-jerk aversion reactions into object lessons in mindfulness.

"What is life but the angle of vision?" Waldo asked. "Life consists in what a man is thinking about all day" (*NHI*). Our worlds are delimited by the angle at which we look at objects, and this angle determines what we take to be real. The things we focus on come to define us. In the case of my anxious student, her preoccupation with abandonment shrinks her vision into that of a frightened child when she feels uncertainty. Writing helps her to step back from this picture, examine her perspective, and reduce the impact of destructive emotions. She is learning to see through her illusions by sharpening her angle of vision, proving Waldo's assertion that "the same world is a Hell, and a Heaven," depending on how you look at it. Our task is to pay attention to how we create our own suffering through "mis-seeing" and to question how we look at things. For example, do you perceive the world through loving or mistrustful eyes? Do you project family traumas onto those around you? Are you adversarial or compassionate, defensive or open to new information? Do you look for the best or the worst in people, and how willing are you to change your opinions? Finally, do you trust your inner guidance, or do you defer to outside opinions?

Waldo came to see that his own missteps resulted from trying to imitate others. "All the mistakes I make arise from forsaking my own station and trying to see the object from another's point of view," he wrote in his journal.[2] This does not mean you can't empathize with or learn from other people, of course. But you don't confuse your own point of view with peripheral perspectives. Abdicating responsibility for your angle of vision, blaming others for your mistakes, only deepens self-deception.

Your vision of the world reflects more about you than it mirrors objective reality. "The reason why the world lacks unity, and lies broken and in heaps, is because man is disunited in himself," after all (*N*). Societies are made up of individuals who are largely blind to their own illusions, doomed to repeat their destructive patterns till they learn to change how they see and think. Fortunately, nature provides us with the hardware for doing just that.

Your Brain Is Plastic

As a child growing up in rural Alabama, Trisha Mitchell had no idea that changing her perspective could save her life. The youngest daughter of an unmarried, twenty-two-year-old mother of six, Trisha was a lissome, cheerful, blue-eyed girl who survived repeated traumas in her childhood home. Sexually abused by her stepfather before the age of ten, Trisha was sworn to secrecy under penalty of death. She subsisted in a state of terrorized hypervigilance familiar to survivors of childhood abuse, trapped in a parallel universe, powerless in a world where no one would save her.

"For a long time, I didn't know there was another way to live," Trisha tells me when I visit her at her home in St. Petersburg, Florida. We're sitting on the patio of her mission-style home, surrounded by vines of orange hibiscus. It's difficult to discern that victimized girl in the radiant sixty-eight-year-old woman Trisha has become, with her shining turquoise eyes and dimpled smile. As Trisha tells me her story, I struggle to bridge the ontological gap between the charming woman sitting before me sipping red wine—self-possessed, sophisticated—and the hardscrabble girlhood that almost killed her. As fortune would have it, Trisha managed to escape that Alabama town and create successful careers as a fashion model, painter, and interior designer. What I want to know is how she managed to emerge from this devastating background with her body, mind, and spirit intact? After carefully considering my question, Trisha looks me in the eye and says, "I paid attention to what was beautiful."

"Can you say more?"

"I learned to see in a different way," she tells me. "When I started painting, the lens that I saw myself through changed. I was no longer a victim or the little girl who was sexually abused but the woman with a paintbrush and the power to transform. Through each stroke, I tell my truth. It's my visual language of color. The art pieces are bridges to my emotional healing."

Splashing indigo, scarlet, or chartreuse onto her canvases, Trisha could feel her experience of reality changing, healing slowly, in a process she has trouble describing in words. This altered filter helped her to update her story, not by imposing rose-colored glasses, but by reminding Trisha that "light in some form or other—color—is always present in the darkest moments." Eventually, with the help of a good therapist, she was able to step out of her black-and-white trauma narrative, knowing this victim tale need not define her or set the course for the rest of her life. The trauma specialist Bessel van der Kolk writes that the ability to change their story is what separates people who are able to heal from trauma and those who aren't.[3] Trisha Mitchell has proved this in her own life. Her refusal to stay trapped in a victim narrative, swamped by self-pity and regret, has helped her to change how she sees. "I feel compassion for that little girl," Trisha tells me. "But I'm not her anymore. Her story doesn't defeat me the way it once did."

Our brain's ability to rewire itself through practice, known as neuroplasticity, proves what philosophers and sages have claimed for millennia: that evolution is an ongoing process and the brain can be reshaped through intention. Shifting habitual thoughts and behaviors accelerates neuroplasticity. Contrary to the fallacy that we're born with a fixed number of brain cells that only diminish over time, the human body actually produces around one hundred thousand new brain cells a day until we die. Our organism is programmed for transformation. Reflective practices such as meditation and expressive writing are especially good for increasing positive change. A number of large studies using long-term meditators reveal startling improvements in brain connectivity in regions associated with concentration, compassion, equanimity, and happiness.[4]

It's no great surprise that positive thoughts should lead to cognitive flexibility, increased attention span, faster processing, and a shift of focus from "me" to "we"; or that negative thinking decreases coordination and balance, and impairs our ability to work with others. Waldo warned against fake positivity (more on this later), yet it can't be denied that positive thinking offers superior fuel for growth. The more you focus on negative thoughts, the more neurons and synapses your brain creates to support these negative thought processes.[5] This is why, when it comes to personal growth, bad frequently leads to worse. Waldo pointed this out with a striking image. "There are those who have the instinct of a bat, to fly against every lighted candle and put it out," he wrote (CL). Anticipating disaster, seeking imperfection, and focusing on mistakes and dissatisfaction lead you to see "as through a glass darkly," to miss out on the brighter view.

Increasing your awareness of this tendency makes it easier to resist the pull of dark thoughts. You learn to follow the sequence from perception to action to self-created reality; mindfulness helps you become less reactive, less subject to the tyranny of mentation. In the Dhammapada, which Waldo knew well, the Buddha described this law of causation.

> Mind is the forerunner of all things.
> If one speaks or acts with an impure mind
> Suffering follows, like the wheel that follows the foot
>   of the ox.

> Mind is the forerunner of all things.
> If one speaks or acts with a pure mind
> Happiness follows, like the shadow that never leaves.[6]

Deprived of self-awareness, we'd be trapped in our conditioned responses, brainwashed by our own beliefs, and unaware of the internal witness whose wider perspective can liberate the mind.

Coming to know this witness awareness is critical to self-reliance, as I've said. This witnessing faculty is associated with metacognition, the brain's ability to think *about* our thoughts and feelings, and observe ourselves from the outside in. The internal witness makes it possible to dispel our own fictions and engage in what Waldo termed "lowly listening," attuning ourselves to inner guidance. When we interrupt our habitual thought patterns, our brains are changed automatically; in fact, every shift in cognition alters how the brain functions.[7] "The mind, stretched to a new idea, never returns to its old dimension," Waldo reportedly said. The Stoics were alert to neuroplasticity and the working of the internal witness as well. In the words of Marcus Aurelius, "The things you think about determine the quality of your mind. Your soul takes on the color of your thoughts."[8]

Witnessing points you back to yourself as the arbiter of truthful inquiry. In fact, the truth exists in each of our minds already, Waldo suggested, and needs only to be brought into conscious awareness. Writing is an incomparable tool for doing so. Putting inchoate thoughts and feelings on paper changes your brain and also teaches you how to live.

Write It Down

Waldo's journal was his closest companion beginning at age fourteen. He called his "commonplace book" The Wide World, and it afforded him the private space in which to survey his inner landscape, to explore the mysteries of his own being. Waldo valued this practice so highly that one of his first questions on meeting Henry David Thoreau was "Do you keep a journal?" He drew lifelong inspiration from his beloved Montaigne, whose unsparing journal reflections became integral to his classic *Essais*. Though Waldo lacked Montaigne's shamelessness—erectile dysfunction and toilet habits were never part of his literary wheelhouse—he aspired to a comparable transparency in his own personal revelations. By examining his character from as many angles as possible, and reporting truthfully on what he observed, he sought to untangle his heart and mind in the pages of The Wide World.

Journal writing is an accessible, catalytic tool on the path of personal discovery. The extensive benefits of expressive writing are startling, in fact. As little as fifteen minutes a day of self-directed writing has been shown to significantly reduce stress, increase immune function, decrease chronic pain, improve emotional intelligence, accelerate wound healing, and lower the incidence of anxiety and depression.[9] Putting words to internal experience is known to reduce absenteeism from work, increase happiness levels, raise grade point averages, improve sporting performance, and elevate our social skills, according to James Pennebaker, a pioneering psychologist in the field of expressive writing.[10] Taking the time to look within and expose what is hidden there *to ourselves*, we relieve the pressure of rumination and make way for positive change. Just as commiserating with a trusted friend can improve your mood when you're feeling lousy, externalizing hidden turmoil can defuse conflict and provide the emotional distance necessary for insight to occur.

I discovered the power of journal writing during my own difficult childhood. Growing up in a family where violence and loss were ever present, I turned inward at an early age for the comfort and guidance that were absent around me. Starting in the third grade, I began to pour my confusion, sadness, and hurt into a journal, discovering that although outer conditions might not change, I always felt better after I wrote. A modicum of clarity replaced the confusion. Discerning the reasons behind my feelings, I could make out how they colored my thoughts. This secret journal became my testing ground, my refuge, the only place where the unsayable things could be spoken. I could step back, connect the dots, resolve conflicts, and even learn from my mistakes. Journaling calls forth the witness that helps you find your way home when you're lost.

Writing also helps you discover meaning where none seemed to exist. Humans are meaning-seeking animals; without a sense of purpose, we lose direction, stamina, and the will to persist. Our need to find meaning in life is comparable to the drives for sex, shelter, and safety, apparently.[11] We carve out meaning by creating stories, including the narrative of what our lives signify. We become more interesting *to ourselves*, investing experience with deeper value. The pen or keyboard becomes our spelunker's light, guiding us into the cave of our mind, illuminating what we uncover. One of the first things a perceptive journaler notices, if she's paying attention, is that this singular person she calls herself is elusive, polyphonic, illusory. Rather than finding some Wizard of Oz, orchestrating life from behind the mind's curtain, she finds a shifting composite, impressions, memories, expectations, projections, opinions, and myths, masquerading as an autonomous "I." Writing helps her penetrate this narrative mask and expose the larger Self behind it.

Beyond the "Me Story"

Waldo taught that beyond the limits of personality there exists a Self, a spiritual presence, that transcends time, place, and biography. This metaphysical intelligence exceeds the limits of a person's conscious awareness manyfold. Realizing that the personality you've taken to be your Self is actually a fraction of your true identity is an important step toward self-reliance.

Waldo encourages us to pull back the narrative curtain and acquaint ourselves with this inner "giant." We must not be deceived by self-limiting stories into forgetting the "infinitude of the private man." Mistaking the bric-a-brac of material life for all that we are, we forget our essential nature and the vast consciousness that contains us. This universal error goes to the heart of our malaises; entranced by superficial offerings, we mistake the tinsel of stuff for the gold of self-knowledge. Our confusion turns us into pretenders, devotees of an image-obsessed culture that profits from our ignorance. The ubiquity of "imposter syndrome," characterized by feelings of fakeness and shame, attest to this confusion. In societies where the existence of our spiritual identity is denied, a concerted, ongoing effort is required for us to break free of this brainwashing.

It's helpful to understand how the self-story becomes so

entrenched. At around eighteen months old, babies begin to perceive themselves as separate entities, autonomous subjects in a world of other subjects, some of whom are nurturing while others oppose them. The toddler becomes aware of herself in a different way through this assumed separation, leading to what Albert Einstein described as an "optical delusion of consciousness."

> This delusion is a kind of prison for us, restricting us to our personal desires and affections for a few persons nearest us. . . . [The child] experiences himself, his thoughts and feelings, as something separated from the rest.[12]

As language develops, the child composes stories to describe, to reify, the objectified *me* she takes to be her true self. Individuation continues with each insistence that the girl is *this* but not *that*. With each negation, another imaginary boundary is laid down between her *self* and *not-self*; the child is further isolated, stumbling further toward inauthenticity. This story serves to make sense of her existence, while splitting her identity into opposing factions of good-bad, permissible-taboo, either-or, and us-them, and concealing her original wholeness. This narrating, labeling, binary process helps her shape a version of herself that is likely to earn her love and acceptance (hence the formation of the psychological shadow), and prevent expulsion from the group. By the time she reaches adulthood, these stories have hardened into a carapace, a fixed identity, adhering like gauze strips on a papier-mâché doll, solid-seeming on the outside but hollow within, forever lacking, not quite real. Thus, the seeds of the imposter syndrome are sown.

Waldo knew that the stories we tell ourselves are bound to harden (when they go unquestioned) into an egotistical prison. He was also aware that most people care little about rending the veils of personal illusion to reveal who they are beyond their me-story. In the *Matrix* of contemporary life, a minority choose the red pill of revelation over the blue pill of complacency. Unexpected life changes, particularly painful ones, can be a boon on the path of self-reliance for this very reason. *Catastrophe* comes from the Greek word for "to turn around"; crisis makes it harder to hide from the truth, which is how it accelerates personal growth. When you lose your cherished fictions, you're forced to look beyond your standard me-story for fresh perspectives and possibilities, to consider the world through sober eyes. Hardship is a springboard to increased authenticity when you use it correctly. Seeing your narrative come apart before your eyes proves how arbitrary your personal fictions are. The self-narrating impulse stands out in relief, showing how your mind creates stories reflexively, as birds produce songs and apples grow out of an apple tree. You recognize these fictions *as fictions*, which also gives you the freedom to change them.

When you integrate your spiritual identity into the character you play in the world, you perceive yourself as personal *and* transcendental. You are both unique and inextricably connected to all sentient beings on this planet. As hybrid creatures, in other words, we can never be contained in a narrative self. This recognition opens us to the ineffable mystery of our true identity. As Waldo explained,

> The materialist . . . believes his life is solid, [that he] knows where he stands and what he does. Yet how easy it is to show him that he is also a phantom walking and working among phantoms, and that he needs only ask a question or two beyond his daily questions, to find his solid [self] growing dim and impalpable before his sense. (*T*)

Breaking through the ceiling of our fixed self-sense, we gain access to the bigger view. No longer rigidly identified with our stories, we're able to play different characters in the world with greater élan and imagination, knowing our composed selves do not define us. We become far less afraid of losing face or sacrificing our reputations.

Transcending her fictions allows a person to see herself as a being in progress, a verb instead of a noun, a shape-shifting individual instead of a papier-mâché personality layered over with intractable stories. While endowed with a measure of personal will, she realizes that she's subject to universal laws and forces infinitely beyond her reckoning. While she might appear solid to the naked eye, closer examination reveals her to be fluid and ever-changing. This fluency changes her self-image and how she relates to her own mind. It becomes self-evident that she does not control her thoughts, though self-inquiry can certainly steady her in the mental torrent.

I remember an epiphany three decades ago during my first silent meditation retreat. I'd been battling with my thoughts for close to a week, struggling to control my mind by focusing on the breath as the teacher had instructed. I felt frantic, trapped, discouraged, and angry, and wanted only to escape from this horrible Zendo and forget about meditation once and for all. One morning, I skipped the predawn sitting and fled to the woods where no one would see me. Pausing by a stream, I watched the water sliding over moss-grown rocks and spiraling into eddies along the shore. As I sat there in silence, my attention softened, and seemed to withdraw, leaving me somewhere beyond my mind, as if I'd taken a seat on the bank of awareness. Distant thoughts continued to flow in the background, but I was no longer standing chin-deep in the current. I was aware of the gap between thinking and being, and that I was not generating these thoughts; they were bubbling up instead from somewhere else. This experience showed me two things clearly: that the thinking mind has a mind of its own; also, that one needn't drown in the cognitive deluge. This brief interval proved to me once and for all that attempts to control our thoughts are doomed. We can, however, step out of the mind stream and witness its commotion from a calm remove. Knowing you don't create your thoughts helps you not take them so personally. It loosens your grip on the me-story, too, including the grip on your cherished opinions, and makes you more receptive to fresh ideas and opportunities when they arise.

Irrational and Unpredictable

The inability to control our own thoughts is particularly boggling since humans are *rationis capax*, now and then, capable of self-guidance through reason. We are both uniquely equipped to observe our minds (and even make sensible decisions, at times) and woefully powerless over our inherent irrationality and unpredictability. When it comes to the impulses behind our behavior, we're never quite in the driver's seat. Psychologist Jonathan Haidt compares this dilemma to the struggle of a mahout (Reason) astride the stubborn elephant of Emotion.[13] The mahout kicks and screams but cannot force the great pachyderm to go where he wants it to. The ego finds this demoralizing, but the limitations of reason are actually a godsend. Imagine how quickly a defensive, fear-driven ego would tyrannize the mind if reason were omnipotent; how rapidly our inner world would devolve into a full-on dictatorship, banishing subversive thoughts, erasing contradiction, paradox, and nuance from human psychology. Given the choice, such a paranoid ego would eradicate whatever threatens its sovereignty and the status quo; in turn, this would deprive us of the opportunity to evolve, challenge beliefs, resolve ongoing conflicts, drop outdated patterns, or entertain new ideas.

Waldo was aware of the limits of reason and advised us to steward our minds the way we would recalcitrant children, providing guidance, boundaries, and common sense without crushing our spirit. The attempt to bully ourselves with reason kills receptivity and interferes with our higher intelligence. While we may not control our thoughts and feelings, however, we can learn to regulate our responses once the elephant of raw emotion has had its way with us. We're able to produce a mental climate that is open, equable, and self-aware. This remains our psychological ace in the hole, though it isn't easy to achieve. "Not he is great who can alter matter but who can alter my state of mind," Waldo admitted (*TAS*). He prized mental equilibrium and freshness of perspective, and the suppleness necessary for metamorphosis to occur. "There is pleasure in the thought that the particular tone of my mind at this moment may be new in the universe," he wrote, and "that [I can] lead a new life."[14]

This Stoic wisdom has become increasingly elusive in the digital age. The ability to think for ourselves, exercise reason, and stabilize our point of view against the deluge of information technology is more difficult and necessary than ever. Consider our plummeting ability to focus. A Harvard study of 250,000 subjects using an iPhone web app showed that the average attention span of Americans has shrunk to a catastrophic degree. Subjects reported spending 46.9 percent of their waking hours thinking about something other than what they were doing.[15] Knowing that rumination ruins well-being, the connection between attention deficit and growing unhappiness becomes obvious. "A human mind is a wandering mind, and a wandering mind is an unhappy mind," according to the study's lead researcher.[16]

The brain receives on the order of eleven million bits of information per second, apparently most of them repetitive thoughts having little to do with the present moment. In our techno-driven age, wading through this miasma of info bytes, memes, and metadata becomes a daunting task that sabotages our ability to pay attention. Cultural influencers make their fortunes manipulating our emotions and distracting us with trivia. Long before Snapchat, TikTok, and "shiny object syndrome"—the state of distraction brought on by the belief that there is something new worth pursuing—Waldo warned against wasting our attention on trifles. He recommended finding "one well-spent hour a day" (*COI*) to regather our focus, tune in to the witness awareness that knows more than we do. Stepping away from the madding crowd, we make room for this free, disobedient self to navigate oppositional influences with focus and integrity.

⤚❧ THE BRIEF ❧⤙

Perspective creates your reality. The mind's narration interferes with clear seeing. This story-making voice creates an illusion of separateness that must be seen through in order to be fully present. We achieve this clarity through a variety of methods—journaling, meditation, therapy, prayer, self-inquiry—that engage your witness awareness. Self-inquiry prompts neuroplasticity (the ability of the brain to rewire itself through practice) and also helps you escape entrapment inside the "little me" story. Expressive writing is a particularly powerful tool for achieving insight; by putting your thoughts and feelings on paper, you externalize inchoate experience, increase objectivity, and make way for the unbiased witness perspective to emerge. This neutral, observing witness is untroubled by contradiction, knows that you are predictably irrational, paradoxical, contrary, and inconsistent, but does not judge you. Your self-created identity, composed of opposites, represents only part of who you are.

On Nonconformity

Build Your Own World

"To be yourself in a world that is constantly
trying to make you something else is the
greatest accomplishment."

Society Is Not Your Friend

Waldo was allergic to authority in general and convinced that society is not to be trusted. Societies conspire against the welfare of their citizens by undercutting independence, prompting moral decay, and fostering a "smooth mediocrity and squalid contentment" (*SR*). When citizens resist their own sovereignty and the mandate to think for themselves, they become pawns rather than agents of their own destiny. Waldo urged us to reject subjugation.

> Let us . . . hurl in the face of custom, and trade, and office,
> the fact which is the upshot of all history, that there is
> a great responsible Thinker and Actor working wherever a
> man works. The greatest act of morality is therefore to be
> a non-conformist. (*SR*)

This Thinker-Actor (our internal witness) is capable of making its own decisions and commandeering our life conditions. Marcus Aurelius agreed with this stance. "Nothing is so conducive to spiritual growth as this capacity for logical and accurate analysis of everything that happens to us," he wrote.[1] For many who prefer to be told what to do, this can be a heavy lift, as Waldo acknowledged. "The vast majority of men at all times, and even heroes in certain eminent moments are imbeciles, victims of gravity, custom, and fear," he wrote (*POW*). Conformity leaves us prey to our dominant culture regardless of how corrupt that culture might be. We're instructed to avoid the "elegant incognitos" of social groups, parties, and sects "designed to save a man from the vexation of thinking."[2] Waldo maintained that humanity, left to its own devices, will gravitate eventually toward the true and the good, and rejected the pessimism of his Puritan forebears. Nonconformity prompts the natural genius of a freethinking person.

His friend Henry Thoreau was living proof of this dictum. Henry was Waldo's prototype of the liberated, self-reliant individual. Fourteen years Waldo's junior and utterly indifferent to the customs of polite society, Henry was a slight man with melancholy gray eyes, a beak-like nose, and a mess of unkempt, chestnut hair. A sworn bachelor who made up for an unimpressive appearance by assuming an aloof, brusque demeanor, Henry exhibited a general disdain for manners and mores of polite society. Unlike Waldo, he was unselfconscious and unconcerned with what people thought about him. Henry had "not a particle of respect to the opinions of any man or body of men but homage solely to the truth itself," as Waldo wrote in his journal.[3] "Thoreau gives me in flesh and blood . . . my own ethics. He is far more real, and daily practically obeying them, than I."[4] Henry's adamantine trust in his own guidance and determination not to conform or imitate others left Waldo awed and envious. He "walk[ed] abreast with his days and [felt] no shame," Waldo wrote of his friend, "for he does not postpone his life but lives, already."[5]

Live already was Waldo's mantra as well, drawing inspiration from his bed-headed friend. "Know your bone; gnaw it, bury it, unearth it, and gnaw it still," Henry wrote in a letter from Walden Pond,[6] where he'd built a small cabin on Waldo's property. Though Henry was erratic, disagreeable, and frequently rude, no one ever doubted his character or sincerity. "Heaven sometimes hedges a rare character about with ungainliness and odium, as the burr protects the fruit," as Waldo noted.[7] Henry was the man he appeared to be, which was not something you could always say about Waldo, who was sometimes several people at once, many of whom he did not like.

Henry tutored him in simplicity. Thoreau's near-shamanic connection to nature and vast knowledge of her flora and fauna came as a revelation to the older man.

My good friend Henry Thoreau made this else solitary afternoon sunny with his simplicity and clear perceptions. How comic is simplicity in this double-dealing, quacking world.[8]

Thoreau was also prescient about what was to come in our outward-facing, media-obsessed culture, where reliance on external approval too often trumps looking within for answers. "In proportion as our inward life fails, we go more constantly and desperately to the post office," Henry wrote. "You may depend on it, that the poor fellow who walks away with the greatest number of letters, proud of his extensive correspondence, has not heard from himself this long while."[9]

Searching inside for guidance fortifies the spirit. Self-reliance depends on the ability to say no without apology or explanation. Behavioral science confirms the connection between nonconformity and self-realization. Nonconformers tend to be happier, stronger, and higher functioning than those who go along with the crowd. In one study that measured biological responses to the personal threat of saying no to the majority, researchers found that when the goal was to *fit in* with people who might disagree with them, subjects' cardiovascular responses were consistent with the state of *threat*: trembling, rapid heart rate, lowered oxytocin levels. When the subjects' goal was to *be an individual* in a group who might disagree with them, cardiovascular responses were consistent with *challenge*: improved blood flow, cardiac efficiency, increased oxytocin. In other words, wellness depends on whether a person is motivated by fear of nonacceptance or driven by the desire to stand up for her own beliefs. "The experience of challenge is more like feeling invigorated than overwhelmed," writes one of the study's authors. "It is consistent with seeing something to gain rather than focusing on what can be lost."[10]

Still nonconformity comes at a cost. It's harder to swim against the tide even when doing so can yield great benefits. In another experiment that focused on group pressure, data showed that when people were encouraged to agree with incorrect information, to acquiesce to the majority and agree with answers they knew to be wrong, a startling 32 percent of the group caved in to pressure. The human desire to avoid confrontation makes peer pressure even more powerful. We like to think that seeing is believing, but the study's findings show that "seeing is believing what the group tells you to believe."[11] We have a hardwired impulse to keep up appearances, and want others to see us as good, even when being "bad" is frequently better. "Good men must not obey the laws too well," Waldo warned (*POL*). This is reminiscent of John Lewis, the civil rights activist and congressman, who pushed activists to get into "good trouble." Disobedience is crucial in times of injustice. Beleaguered by racial inequality, economic unfairness, and myriad social evils issuing from the top, we learn that nonconformity is essential for maintaining our integrity. But integrity is an inside job, not a performance for others.

Don't Be Too Good

A bearded thirtysomething named Joe discovered this for himself. Joe had been a successful IT engineer when he realized that he had chosen the wrong life. "I felt trapped and it was getting worse," he says.[12] Joe is sitting inside his car in Moab, Utah, explaining why he decided to ditch a promising career and bourgeois lifestyle to become a nomadic wanderer in 2014. Working sixty hours a week at a job that barely covered his living expenses, he realized it was high time he got into some good trouble and focused on following his bliss.

"First, I hiked the Pacific Crest Trail from Mexico to Canada," Joe goes on. "It was something I'd wanted to do for a while." This experience was life-changing and led him to give up his apartment, rent a PO box, and take his show on the road. Joe drove the length and breadth of the United States over the next year, in search of wide open spaces and new kinds of people beyond the bounds of his corporate job. Breaking the rules and obeying his impulses changed Joe profoundly. "There's a saying out here, that hiking will ruin your life in the best possible way," he says. "I definitely found that to be the case for myself."

By standing up to the people in his life who warned him that he was making a mistake, Joe began to feel "more independent and more connected" at the same time. Questioning the "work first, life second" refrain of the American dream, he was surprised to discover that he had been free all along. "It turns out there are really no rules on how a person has to live," he says. "I wanted to have more time *much* more than I wanted more money." He pauses to let this sink in. "Believe it or not, you don't need to pay rent to have a place to sleep." Joe now alternates between camping, housesitting, living in his car, and spending time in spectacular locations like this campsite near Arches National Park.

Along the way, he's getting to know himself better. "It's been easier and simpler than I expected. More versatile, too." Joe's no-madic lifestyle has forced him to "get real," pare down his needs, and live more honestly, closer to the land. "What I tell people who are thinking of doing this, is, don't try to replicate your old life when you're on the road." This is an essential point. "You can't stuff a three-bedroom house into a minivan. Let things be new. Trust that what you'll find out here is different. And chances are, it'll be a whole lot better."

To be a nonconformist means dropping our fixation on being seen as a "good" people. In a Christian nation fueled by the myth that we're all born sinners, this is a tall order. Weaned on the toxic doctrine of being fallen creatures because we inhabit animal bod-ies, we're conditioned to doubt ourselves. "He who would gather immortal palms must not be hindered by the name of goodness but must explore if it is goodness," Waldo warned (*SR*). He de-tested virtue signaling, as it's known today, and was vigilant to society's reflexive attempts to manipulate the conscience of its cit-izens. Cancel culture thrives on this negative cycle. It assumes the worst of other people, refuses mercy, defines individuals by their worst mistakes, and fosters an ideal of virtue that is untenable and damaging. Waldo would have found this hypocritical, even laugh-able, our habit of posing behind righteous façades, and lobbing shame-grenades at one another, as if we were guiltless. The push to sanitize one's social image is anathema to self-reliance. "Your goodness must have some edge to it, else it is none," he reminds us (*SR*). Also, "a little wickedness is good to make muscle" (*POW*).

Displays of propriety do not make you virtuous. It is how a man lives his daily experience that displays the truth of his character.

Waldo detested sanctimony above all, none more so than that of "good" people who wear virtuous masks in public while being miscreants behind closed doors. Benevolence inveigled by social guilt is harmful to our integrity. He cited the example of public charity, acknowledging the "thousandfold Relief societies" that had cropped up around the country, and warned that if charity doesn't begin in the heart it is a form of moral bribery. "Though I confess with shame I sometimes succumb and give the dollar, it is a wicked dollar which by and by I shall have the manhood to withhold," he confessed (SR). Waldo wasn't railing against generosity, of course, but emphasizing a point about fraudulence. Hypocrisy is perpetuated by conformists doing good for selfish reasons. When "men do what is called a good action, as some piece of courage or charity, much as they would pay a fine in expiation," they betray their integrity. "I do not wish to expiate but to live," he insisted, rejecting the need for penance. "My life is not an apology, but a life" (SR).

It's worth asking yourself how often you apologize for your choices—and your life. How much time and energy do you waste in worrying about other people's opinions? Do you label yourself a sinful person, while pretending to be better than you are? These are helpful questions to consider when thinking about your approach to goodness. Overconscientiousness is a bad sign in a person (like "sticking at gnats"), Waldo believed. No one likes a Goody Two-Shoes. Picayune adherence to nonsensical rules and flourishes of public virtue do not constitute righteousness. Waldo insisted that false displays of benevolence often signal that worse offenses are being covered up. Authentic conscience is the result of locating the virtue within.

Whence is your power? Where does my authority lie? From my non-conformity. I never listened to your people's law or to what they call their gospel and wasted my time. I was content with the simple rural poverty of my own, hence this sweetness. (*CHA*)

Majority rule should never override your innate sense of equality and justice, especially since consensus reality is so changeable and arbitrary, limited by time, place, and culture. It's up to the individual to be a nonconformist when society contradicts what she knows to be right. In other words, you must trust your own experience first. "No law can be sacred to me but that of my own nature," Waldo explained. "The only right is what is after my constitution; the only wrong is what is against it" (*SR*).

He counseled radical acceptance for the choices we've made, and a wide berth when it comes to tolerating our own contradictions. Inconsistency is a virtue, not a tragic flaw, and, "a foolish consistency is the hobgoblin of little minds," as he famously wrote (*SR*). There are no straight lines in nature, after all; life proceeds incrementally, by mysterious ways. "The voyage of the best ship is a zigzag of a hundred tacks," he reminds us (*SR*). Nature's rhythms are contrapuntal, syncopated, offbeat; she expands and contracts, rises and falls, begins and pauses, in the exuberant natural process of thriving. It's impossible to subdivide reality into tidy columns as on an Excel spreadsheet; contradictoriness is forever baked into the human equation.

This is an essential point. We can't respond wisely to life's shifting demands when we focus on consistency over spontaneity.

We're "predictably irrational" in our behavior for crucial reasons (nonconformity and irrationality are deeply linked).[13] In the words of one philosopher, "An ape that in any circumstances conceives of a banana as the highest good will be at a constant disadvantage to a creature that is able to assess the importance of a banana depending on the circumstances."[14] The same is true of human inconsistency. To be overly predictable in an unpredictable world is a deadly disadvantage; habit can easily blind a person to critical changes on the ground. Waldo recommended rebelliousness as a countermeasure for balancing this herdlike mandate to behave, fit in, and repeat ourselves. The rebel is the youth within us, the irrepressible spiritual child.

Be Youthful and Impetuous

The virtues of youth—spontaneity, flexibility, curiosity, gumption, eagerness for new beginnings—are precious and must be protected, Waldo taught. The young are far more likely *not* to take no for an answer because somebody, somewhere, for reasons that may or may not be valid, laid down the law for generations to come.

Creativity—including the art of becoming oneself—requires a willingness to move *toward* the unknown rather than away from it. Without boundary-pushing, impetuousness, and risk-taking, no one can fulfill her potential nor bring her original ideas to fruition. Waldo glorified youthful fecundity, an ideal that is found across spiritual traditions. The mystic child has been celebrated throughout the ages as an archetype of freedom and efflorescence. When

we trust this untutored part of ourselves, we come of age spiritually; "the Child is father of the Man," as Wordsworth wrote.[15] The
child-self embodies evolutionary growth and the guileless directness children possess before curiosity has been dulled by habit,
authenticity erased by obedience. Youthfulness brings openness,
vitality, and hunger for experience; it also engenders receptivity to
mystery and revelation. In Matthew 18:3, Jesus explains to his followers, "Truly I tell you, unless you change and become like little
children, you will never enter the kingdom of heaven." Unless we
retain a measure of innocence, and cultivate what Zen Buddhists
call "beginner's mind," we lose touch with our higher intelligence
and the native truth of who we are. Till we drop the know-it-all
mask of adulthood, we cannot enjoy the fullness of being.

Waldo fixated on the spiritual value of youthfulness, in part,
because he never experienced it in childhood. There's a wistfulness
in Waldo's writing about youth, knowing what we do about his
seriousness as a boy, his premature burden of responsibility. This
yearning for impetuousness contributed as well to his odd-couple
attraction to Henry. Waldo longed for the extroversion of his
brothers and peers, their spirited willingness to flaunt the rules.
"These seething brains, these admirable radicals, these unsocial
worshippers, these talkers who talk the sun and moon away," were
enviable to him (T). He believed youthful insouciance is necessary for us to blossom as adults. "When duty whispers low, 'Thou
must,' the young replies, 'I can.'" After all, "Only to the youth will
spring the spring." He wrote that "passion rebuilds the world for
the youth," and "makes all things alive and significant" (COU).

Nature instructs us to be youthful, bendable, unencumbered
by the past.

> A man casts off his years as a snake its slough, and at
> whatever period soever in life, is always a child in the
> woods, is perpetual youth. (*N*)

Childlike enthusiasm—a word deriving from the Greek for "filled with God"—links us to the electrifying, verdant power of eros, termed *veriditas* by the thirteenth-century German mystic Hildegard of Bingen. Contact with the evergreen force of the universe revivifies the individual, helps her to thrive, and fends off the inertia that increases with age. Choosing evolution over submission, we dive into the unspooling flow of the future, which is bound to oppose the traditional current. "This one fact the world hates, that the soul becomes; for that forever degrades the past, turns all riches to poverty," Waldo writes (*SR*). Nature contradicts social stasis in her extravagant refusal to stop evolving; she simply will not be frozen in place. Life's verdancy always appeals to the future. A person who aspires to self-reliance (and excellence) must turn her back on what's dead and gone, and resist the urge to cling to the past. She learns to cultivate youthfulness, motility, joy, and gladness at being alive. Poet E. E. Cummings echoed this sentiment beautifully:

> You shall above all things be glad and young
> For if you're young, whatever life you wear
> it will become you; and if you're glad
> whatever's living will yourself become.[16]

Such gladness fuels the fountain of youth, heals us of the need to be "good," and drops the mantle of shame from our shoulders. We relinquish the need to be popular, too, or impress others with our extraordinary charms.

Popularity Is for Dolls

In this era of competitive popularity (how may hearts did you get on Insta today?), it's hard to resist the siren call of ingratiation in our campaign to make friends and influence people. The titans of social media profit off of this insatiable need for attention, tailoring their algorithms to feed the hunger for clicks, pings, and kissy emoticons. Many resemble adolescents perched breathlessly at their keyboards, waiting to find out if they're "in" or "out" that day, celebrated or forgotten.

This popularity industrial complex exacerbates the "fallacy of insignificance" that Colin Wilson wrote about seventy-five years ago, in which the average person "has been conditioned by society to lack self-confidence in his ability to achieve anything of real worth."[17] In an effort to escape feelings of worthlessness, he imitates others' strategies for success while hiding aspects of himself that could threaten acceptance in the public square. Waldo would have been appalled by this copycat culture that has turned us into a nation of voracious voyeurs, desperately struggling to believe that we matter. Waldo recognized this incipient danger in his own time ("Most men feel like gnats on the ass of society," he wrote somewhere) but could hardly have predicted its destructiveness in the age of social media.

When Apple announces its newest miracle gadget, customers

camp out en masse on the sidewalk to make sure they don't miss out. Such status symbols are intended to boost consumers' self-esteem but often leave them feeling needier, and less confident, than before. Writer Andrew Harvey assesses this con game clearly. "Modern culture feeds off an anxiety and depression it carefully nurtures with a consumer machine that must keep us greedy and insecure for its own survival," he writes. Harvey likens victims of consumerism to "people crawling through an endless desert, dying of thirst, and all this culture holds out to us is a drink of saltwater designed to make us thirstier."[18]

Nonconformity is a potent weapon against such manipulation. "Envy is ignorance, imitation is suicide," Waldo wrote (*SR*). Also, "popularity is for dolls" (*CUL*). It's a bad idea to dumb yourself down to be in sync with the lowest common denominator. "If you try to be something you're not . . . you end up a pathetic dabbler," Epictetus observed in first-century Athens.[19] Shamelessness, an underestimated virtue in spiritual life, is needed to help us reject convention in favor of self-reliance. Stripped of self-consciousness and the urge to compete, we benefit our spiritual lives at the expense of the preening ego. While popularity may take a hit, we free ourselves of the need to impress.

We've learned as much from history's spiritual exemplars, shameless men and women (frequently represented as tricksters or fools), who've stepped outside the moral matrix to claim their freedom. Diogenes of Sinope, who predated Epictetus by several centuries, refused to cover his naked body, shamelessly parading his business before man and God while residing in a tub on a public street. Diogenes was a founder of the Cynic school of philosophy, which celebrated shamelessness (*avaioeia*) as a way of opposing the *nomos* of society: the laws, customs, and social conventions that citizens take for granted but are arbitrary.

Waldo's shamelessness, unlike Henry's, was concealed beneath a mask of Yankee reserve. In the privacy of his mind, he was an orgiast of transgression and risk. "I wish to break all prisons," he confessed in his journal, "[but] I have not yet conquered my own house."[20] The world "whips [a nonconformist] with its displeasure" (*SR*), but the urge to people-please must be resisted. An example of this from Waldo's own life came in the aftermath of his incendiary Harvard Divinity School address (which we'll talk about later) when he was not only unrepentant but delighted to have caused such a scandal. "It seems very clear to me that if I live, my neighbors must look for a great many more shocks and perhaps harder to bear," he gloated. Rejecting the pleas of trusted advisers, who "importun[ed]" Waldo with "the dear old doctrines of the Church, and begged him to save his immortal soul through contrition," he stood firm. "What have I to do with the sacredness of traditions, if I live wholly from within?"[21] The incendiary address that got him barred from Harvard's campus for decades was Waldo's spiritual declaration of independence. It is possible to remain yourself regardless of outside influences, he tells us.

> It is easy in the world to live after the world's opinion; it is easy in solitude to live after our own; but the great man is he who in the midst of the crowd keeps with perfect sweetness the independence of solitude.[22]

The French call this quality *je m'en foutisme*, the shameless refusal to give a damn about propriety. This quality is teachable, fortunately; the most conventional person can learn to defy convention and follow the dictates of her heart. When Joe the nomad tore up his lease and ignored the advice of peers, he was exercising the muscle of *je m'en foutisme*.

When Henry leapfrogged social propriety, as he frequently did, often to the horror of those who knew him, he was giving voice to his shameless spirit. We must become conscious of our own shame before we can transcend it, however, which takes patience, courage, and strength. Destructive shame infects and hobbles our lives (as opposed to healthy shame, which serves a positive social purpose, resulting from some misdeed or doing harm). Self-forgiveness is needed to heal toxic shame and free ourselves of self-consciousness.

To his dying day, Henry remained Waldo's role model of a happy-to-be-unpopular person. After Henry's death from tuberculosis at forty-four, Waldo didn't mince words in his eulogy. He admitted that Henry's virtues "sometimes ran to extremes," and his "dangerous frankness" had earned him the nickname "that terrible Thoreau." Waldo reminded Henry's mourners that his friend had

> bred to no profession; he never married; he lived alone; he never went to church; he never voted; he refused to pay a tax to the state; he ate no flesh, he drank no wine, he never knew the use of tobacco.... He had no temptations to fight against—no appetites, no passions, no taste for elegant trifles.[23]

Henry was consistently inconsistent, which is how he managed to stay so honest. His personality was challenging but also organic, growing out of his rough-hewn character. Nature is complex and many-sided, prone to paradoxical extremes, just like human beings. Paradox is pervasive in our universe, which is why it dominated Waldo's teaching.

❧ THE BRIEF ❧

To be free, you must be a nonconformist. A nonconformist resists the urge to give her power away to others; she refuses to sacrifice who she is for the sake of popularity. Society is not your friend as its purpose is to protect its own existence. Society is the enemy of nonconformists. It's crucial to examine why and when you're obedient and not tailor your conscience to fit the fashion of the times. It's a mistake to try to be too good; false virtue (including virtue signaling) helps no one. You can trust your inherent kindness, which naturally prompts generosity toward others. There's nothing worse than a self-righteous prig. You don't want to lose your childlike qualities—the candor, impetuousness, curiosity, stubbornness—that preserve your authenticity. On the path of self-reliance, the hunger to perform for others' approval is harmful, and rendered more addictive in our TikTok'ing times.

On Contradiction

Everything Is Double

"There is a crack in everything God has made."

Working with Paradox

Waldo applied Isaac Newton's Third Law of Motion—"for every action in nature there is an opposite and equal reaction"—to the realm of psychology. For every quality or trait you possess, an opposite and equal attribute exists, which is why it is necessary to accommodate both. Since "our strengths grow out of our weaknesses," the wise person must learn to coexist with her foibles. "No man had ever a point of pride that was not injurious to him, so no man had ever a defect that was not somewhere useful to him." Being many-sided should cause no shame, and "a great man is always willing to be little" (*C*).

Qualities we resist in ourselves may be crucial to our wholeness. Contradictions cause us to rub up against complex reality and are beneficial to personal growth. "Whilst he sits on the cushion of advantages, he goes to sleep," Waldo noted of the average person. "When he is pushed, tormented, defeated, he has a chance to learn something" (*C*). Understanding that paradox fosters strength, and accepting that "there is a crack in everything God has made" (*C*) defeats our attempts to be monolithic and helps us reconcile our cloven nature. The tension of opposites gives us backbone; whining over flaws and inconsistencies is a colossal waste of time. It's far better to get off our high horse and accept the conditions we've been given.

When an Episcopal priest named Andrea Martin was a child being treated for LLD—a condition in which one limb is longer than the other—bedtime was the most painful time of day. "I would lie there till morning came, crunched up in agony," Andrea tells me when I visit her at the rectory in Connecticut where she is the junior pastor. Feisty, self-deprecating, and extremely smart (she's a graduate of the Yale Divinity School), Andrea is a petite woman with pixie hair and a pronounced limp who endured fifteen major surgeries as a girl, spending six months out of every year trapped inside a body cast. She suffered through numerous excruciating leg-lengthening surgeries and these rack-like procedures continued till the age of twenty-one.

"The emotional pain was worse than the physical pain," says Andrea. "My mother used to say, 'Andrea, your struggle right now is very difficult on the outside. But everybody has challenges and hurts and struggles that are not always so visible,'" wisdom that eventually led her to her vocation as a priest. "There's a huge amount of pressure on people to have it all together, or to look like it at least, even when they're crumbling inside," she continues. "My job is to look past the exterior into somebody's heart and soul, knowing that what's inside can be very different from what they present."

Much of her clergy work involves helping parishioners to reconcile their mismatched parts and recognize how their weaknesses, fears, and missteps contribute to their singular wholeness. Andrea explains that imagination plays an integral part in this healing process. As an illustration, she tells me about a doctor friend, an artist in his off-hours, who makes one-of-a-kind sculptures out of discarded junk from the hospital where he works—old x-ray film, IV tubing, gauze, broken casts—proving that nothing need be wasted in this imperfect life, no matter how useless it may seem. "That's a great metaphor for hope and how God acts on our behalf," Andrea explains. "It's like found art. You take all the bad things—the pain, the embarrassment, anger, longing—also surprising moments of grace—and form them into something original and unique which then becomes your life." When we incorporate our broken parts and "collaborate with this creative, redemptive spirit, amazing things can happen," as she knows from painful experience.

In a nation where perfectionism is a cultural pastime, encouraging us to hold ourselves to impossible standards, paradox and contradiction are rarely viewed so generously. Our difficulty with tolerating contradiction is linked to a distinct cultural bias. In a study comparing American and Chinese attitudes toward complexity, researchers found that East Asians have a higher capacity for reconciling seemingly incompatible opposites, as their view of reality is inherently paradoxical.[1] According to the study's authors, Americans tend toward binary thinking and find it more difficult to tolerate ambiguity. "Americans want to work out which side is 'right,'" they found, failing to appreciate that right and wrong are relative cultural valuations. The Eastern bias, on the other hand, is *dialectical*, a nuanced approach that endeavors to preserve the basic elements of opposing perspectives while locating a middle way. Americans err on the side of logic; in social science, this is called a *differentiation* model, meaning an orientation that polarizes contradictory perspectives in an effort to determine which is more correct. We see a glaring example of this binary, differentiation style in the Washington gridlock handicapping the nation, wherein the mandate to be right often outweighs the civic obligation to serve the public.

The Asian bias is wiser and more effective in a globalized, increasingly diverse world where conditions change 24/7 and opposites will always exist. On an individual level, Waldo encourages us to accept our dialectical selves for the sake of authenticity. "Every man in his lifetime needs to *thank* his faults" (my emphasis), he insists (*C*). This is easier said than done, of course. How can a person feel gratitude for qualities in herself she finds obnoxious or embarrassing, attributes that cause her grief and make her feel like an outsider? How is it possible to turn flaws into allies, optimize our paradoxes, and "turn lemons into lemon chiffon," as a baker friend of mine puts it?

I was confronted by such a conundrum myself as a lonely kid

desperate to connect but having none of the standard tools of attraction. Shy, underprivileged, and suspicious of others, I came
to discover that by asking questions, expressing interest in people
who'd otherwise ignore me, I was able to draw them to me and
feel that I was needed. I learned that people longed to tell their
stories—if only someone would listen—and played the part of a
pint-sized reporter, urging others to reveal themselves, persuad-
ing neighbors, acquaintances, and semi-strangers to reveal their
secrets to me in private. This strategy worked surprisingly well; I
never seemed to run out of questions or interest in knowing what
made people tick. An inquisitiveness born of alienation became
a genuine asset later as a journalist, where I specialized in inter-
viewing difficult subjects, and later as a memoir writer, when I
could turn this flair for interrogation back on myself. Eventually,
this need to ask questions, to uncover the truth behind social
masks, led to my creating a writing method that helps others explore their secret stories and tell the truth about who they are.

In other words, a neurotic, obsessive quality that might have
turned me into the town drunk, buttonholing strangers at the
bar, became something of value in my life. I saw how a painful
personal weakness could be turned into an asset, as Waldo taught.

> Every excess causes a defect; every defect an excess. Every
> sweet has its sour; every evil its good. Every faculty which is a
> receiver of pleasure has an equal penalty put on its abuse. (C)

In himself, he had channeled his extreme introversion, his
"porcupine impossibility of contact," into a writer's vocation,

safeguarding the emotional distance he needed in order to observe human nature with such astounding clarity, from a philosophical remove. Waldo created strengths from weaknesses throughout his life; even after Ellen's death, in the depths of his grief and loneliness, he discovered a "lightness and freedom" that also buoyed him, as he wrote to Aunt Mary. Transformation *through* paradox is possible when you utilize the power of compensation.

The Other Is You

In our polarized world, paradox reveals that beyond the binary of us-versus-them is a third possibility (self-transcendence) that can neutralize irreconcilable opposition. Waldo warned that over-identification with one's groups and its opinions leads only to ignorance and ongoing conflict. When in-groups are formed, out-groups are created automatically; the tribal war drums start beating, and no one escapes unbloodied. Jewish theologian Martin Buber describes this dilemma: "With the words us versus them the world is divided in two [between] the children of light and the children of darkness, the sheep and the goats, the elect and the damned."[2]

For much of human history, it was best to assume the worst of strangers and outside groups. Social "othering" helped our species survive, which is why tribalism is so deeply appealing. But group narcissism and self-favoritism have long outlasted their usefulness. Us-versus-them is our most crushing ethical albatross in a nuclear world. The notion that others are less deserving of everything than we are, simply because *they are not us*, is an artifact that must be discarded. Yet our tendency to "other" also has a paradoxical upside: enemy-making rendered intergroup cooperation mandatory if humans were to survive as a species. Our belligerence necessitated social intelligence and the invention of ethics and morality. As primatologist Frans de Waal puts it, "Humankind's noblest achievement—morality—has evolutionary ties to our basest behavior . . . warfare. . . . The sense of community required by the former was provided by the latter."[3]

Group loyalty is a two-edged sword in any case, and Waldo's views on civil disobedience grew out of this awareness. Pledging loyalty to corrupt social systems is corrupting, as I've said, making it necessary to challenge societal demands and weigh them against individual values. Self-reliance requires us to balance civic obedience against private virtue, public decorum against personal conscience. Social roles demand balancing acts that often seem antithetical. This "double consciousness," as Waldo described it—playing different roles in diverse situations depending on the demands of the moment—is demanding and complicated. As social creatures, we're called on daily to alter our postures, styles, and inflections to mirror changing circumstances.

> A man must ride alternately on the horse of his private and public nature, as the equestrians of a circus throw themselves nimbly from horse to horse, or plant one foot on the back of the one, and the other foot on the back of the other. (*F*)

Shape-shifting is necessary and not problematic, provided we know it's happening. Danger arises only when we mistake the act for the acrobat. When we play our parts intentionally, mindful that we're adopting different roles to fulfill alternating responsibilities, this circus act becomes less disorienting. Group loyalty distorts self-image, however, and must be acknowledged in order for us to self-correct. When you're protected by the banner of some group or other, it's easier to be grandiose, to inflate your identity in accordance with your team's status. Group narcissism says that if your group is wonderful, then you must be wonderful for being a member. While few of us are comfortable claiming, "I'm the greatest!" it's perfectly okay to shout about your religion's supremacy or proclaim America to be the greatest country on earth. This marks you as a patriot, not a sociopath.

Psychologist Erich Fromm, who knew a lot about sociopathy as a Jewish refugee from Hitler's Third Reich, explains. "An individual, unless he is mentally very sick, may have at least some doubts about his personal narcissistic image. The member of the group has none, since narcissism is shared by the majority," he wrote.[4] Divided into opposing camps, "the other" is no longer seen as a whole person. Such stereotyping justifies violence and renders enemy-making inevitable. A few weeks after the attacks on 9/11, I interviewed the spiritual teacher Eckhart Tolle, who explained this process incisively. "When people become concepts, it becomes possible to treat them any way we like," Eckhart said, sitting outside his cabin in upstate New York. "It's the label, the concept, that is the cause." He paused for a minute, gazing at the treetops surrounding us. "This is how such atrocities are possible between human beings."

In Waldo's day, the abomination of slavery exemplified this inhumanity on a shocking scale. He had nothing but contempt for this institution.

> I do not see how a barbarous community can constitute a state. I think we must get rid of slavery or we must get rid of freedom. (*CTH*)

W. E. B. Du Bois, the social historian and activist, adopted Waldo's idea of double consciousness to describe the African American experience. "It is a peculiar sensation, double consciousness," wrote Du Bois, "this sense of always looking at one's self through the eyes of others, of measuring one's soul by the tape of a world that looks on in amused contempt or envy."[5] While it is inaccurate to compare a freeborn person's sense of alienation to that of enslaved people, certain psychological parallels can't be denied. Who among us has never felt trapped, confined by an ill-fitting role or persona? Who has never been condescended to by people who deem us inferior or fail to see us for who we are and give us our proper due? It's the rare individual who has never, in some context or other—professional, romantic, intellectual, economic, racial, sexual, religious—felt like a second-class citizen or been pressured to accommodate the majority's wishes. Most everyone knows how it feels to be othered, rejected for who we are, forced to shrink to fit into social niches, to be subjected to microaggressions even when they're couched in humor. Apparently, there is only one universal joke: the us-and-them gag known as a Polish joke. "The Flemish have Walloon jokes," as one researcher writes, "the English tell Irish jokes, the Hutu have Tutsi jokes, and the people of Tokyo have jokes about the people of Osaka."[6] No matter who you are, what you own, or how much power you hold, there will come a time when the other is you. That is when you learn compassion and the Stoic art of turning challenges to your advantage.

Turn the Obstacle Upside Down

Marcus Aurelius writes in *Meditations* that "nature takes every obstacle, every impediment, and works around it—turns it to its purpose, incorporates it into itself." As parts of nature, we have the ability to mimic that process, turning setbacks into opportunities for progress. He continues:

> Our inward power, when it obeys nature . . . turns obstacles into fuel. What's thrown on top of the conflagration is absorbed, consumed by it—and makes it burn still higher. . . . The impediment to action advances action. What stands in your way becomes the way.[7]

This reversal requires critical thinking as well as imagination. The capacity for abstract thought allows us to imagine alternative outcomes and strategies when confronted by adverse conditions. The willingness to shift our perspective determines whether adversity is seen as the enemy or viewed as a potential ally. When hardships are perceived as teachable moments, when our reflexive resistance to adversity is questioned, we're no longer the victims of circumstance. Instead, we become emotional alchemists capable of transforming dark materials into the gold of insight.

Take an ordinary example. You find yourself at a holiday dinner when your least favorite uncle starts spewing his onerous political views, aiming them at you (the volatile liberal) in particular. With each preposterous citing of "fake news," every ludicrous conspiracy theory, your blood pressure steadily rises. If you were alone with this ignoramus, you'd counter his bigoted, fact-free nonsense, but all eyes at the table are on you. If you take the bait and retaliate, which you would relish doing, the remainder of this family dinner is likely to be ruined. Tempers will flair, good humor will crumble. Rather than strike back, however, you remember your Stoic lessons and set about turning the obstacle upside down, to navigate this contretemps with care. You ask yourself, how can I neutralize this combustible moment without throwing a gravy boat at his head? The answer is to focus on the greater good. Surrounded by beloved family members, you contemplate how much your affection for them outweighs your disgust toward this troublemaking fool. The best way to demonstrate this love, you realize, is to exercise patience and self-control, ignore the war drum of political conflict, and take the high road. As your uncle prattles on with his crazy opinions, you're careful to avoid eye contact and proceed slowly toward dessert. The less anger you show, the more rapidly his diatribe fizzles out. Holiday disaster is averted. You're aware of the family's gratitude and respect, and you feel stronger, more self-possessed, for having followed your internal guidance.

"Life invests itself with inevitable conditions, which the unwise seek to dodge," counseled Waldo. "There is always this vindictive circumstance stealing in at us unawares" (C). Luckily, we're not powerless against opposition, knowing we can choose our responses. Bernard of Clairvaux, the eleventh-century Burgundian saint, put it this way: "Nothing can work me damage except myself. The harm that I sustain I carry about with me, and never am a real sufferer but by my own fault."[8] Choice determines outcome, once again, and even the most despicable conditions may prompt surprising insights and wisdom.

In order to choose in this mindful way, it's necessary to pause, step back from your feelings, gauge the situation clearly, ascertain what it means to you, scrutinize your own assumptions—which thoughts are reliable, which are not—and imagine the optimal way forward. How can you resolve the conflict at hand with objectivity, humility, know-how, and humor? How can you flip this challenge on its head to reveal unforeseen, unexpected solutions? Remembering this sovereignty over your responses frees you from reactivity. You learn to modulate your knee-jerk reactions and avoid the damage they can cause.

Flesh and Spirit

No challenge is more paradoxical than untangling our biological, emotional, and spiritual impulses. What the heart desires, the mind often rejects, and what the loins crave may be anathema to the conscience. We're ethical platypuses, living conundrums equipped with mismatched parts and irreconcilable differences. Wisdom is found in the middle way, the Golden Mean, by navigating our disparate faculties with full appreciation of their respective values. But how is it possible to harmonize our discordant tones? Can we create an original composition that truthfully reflects who we are? Or are we bound to be in perpetual conflict, torn between antagonistic desires vying for supremacy? This complex dance between flesh and spirit boggled Waldo as much as the rest of us.

In his personal life, Waldo was a work in progress when it came to matters of carnal freedom. While rejecting the body-negative Christian orthodoxy of his time, he never fully succeeded in silencing Aunt Mary's Calvinist voice in his head, warning him that the body was the source of all evil. According to scripture, one who imagines carnal sin is guilty of that sin already. When eighteen-year-old Waldo confessed to "a nasty appetite which I will not gratify" in his journal, he surely believed masturbation to be the hand of the Devil going where it oughtn't.[9] Nonetheless, he could not deny his romantic, passionate nature, whether rhapsodizing over the charms of women or mooning over a boy in school. A Harvard classmate named Martin Gay appears to have made a special impression. "I begin to believe in the Indian doctrine of eye fascination," Waldo wrote in his journal.

> The cold blue eye of [M] has so intimately connected
> him to my thoughts and visions that a dozen times a day,
> as often by night, I find myself wholly wrapped up in
> conjectures of his character and inclinations. We have

already two or three long profound stares at each other. Be it wise or weak or superstitious, I must know him.[10]

We know nothing of what passed between Waldo and Martin. What we can know for certain is that Waldo developed a lifelong habit, common among the sexually repressed, of gilding the lily of sexual desire with luminous ideals. He resisted carnality for its own sake and shared the Stoics' buzz-killing tendency to look on erotic matters with skepticism. Who can forget Marcus Aurelius's peculiar advice for not getting hooked on sensual pleasure?

> How good it is when you have roast meat . . . before you . . . to impress on your mind, this is the dead body of a fish . . . a bird or pig . . . and your purple-edged robe is simply the hair of sheep soaked in shellfish blood! And in sexual intercourse that it is no more than the function of a membrane and a spurt of mucus ejected.[11]

When Walt Whitman was an unknown poet, he asked Waldo for advice on how to turn his first book, *Leaves of Grass*, into a commercial success after its initial tepid reception. Waldo strongly encouraged him to delete the "Children of Adam" sections, which were homoerotic and unusually graphic, if he hoped to appease his critics (fortunately, Whitman declined this suggestion). Unbridled as he was in the bedroom of his imagination, Waldo was tightly buttoned in real life. Romantic idealism led him to believe that sex without spirit is empty and sad, and that copulation for its own sake is a lowly pursuit. Only when eros is wedded to love can it fulfill its divine purpose, he believed. Left to its own, the thrill-seeking body only leads to disaster. But when sex is a conduit for the heart, it becomes rich with meaning. The animal act becomes a poignant symbol of union when it includes our "higher" faculties.

On the topic of gender and sexual roles, though, he was far ahead of his time. "Hermaphrodite is . . . the symbol of the finished soul," he wrote.[12] Waldo knew that anatomy alone cannot determine an individual's identity, and both femaleness and maleness coexist in us all. A man without awareness of his feminine nature is as half-baked as a woman unfamiliar with her masculine traits. He wrote, "The finest people marry the two sexes in their person," and gravitated in his life toward rebels against conventional gender roles.[13] His passionate friendship with Margaret Fuller was a striking example of this and will be explored in detail later. Margaret had been raised by a father who provided her with the advantages traditionally reserved for men. She was the first woman given entrance to Harvard Library (though she could not enroll as a student). "There is no wholly masculine man [and] no purely feminine woman," Margaret agreed.[14] She brought this radical feminism to their friendship. Margaret's liberated presence thrilled Waldo when he wasn't being put off by her advances. Their friendship was a marriage of opposites that reflected the doubleness they both shared.

Though transsexualism was unknown to him, it seems likely that Waldo would have defended the right of individuals to discover gender for themselves. He was aware that the interplay between flesh and spirit is personal and paradoxical, and that categories overlap in nature. Kate Bornstein, the activist and author of *Gender Outlaw*, puts it this way: "Definitions have their uses in much the same way that road signs make it easy to travel: they point out the directions. But you don't get where you're going when you just stand underneath some sign, waiting for it to tell you what to do."[15] Permitting our disparate parts to emerge, allowing doubleness to be what it is, we enjoy an expanded sense of wholeness that is integrated, polyphonic, and comfortable with paradox. We question wholesale attempts to reduce individuals to labels and roles. As Andrea Martin, the priest with a bad leg, told me, "The spirit itself breaks through the body and creates a story of its own." We gain confidence and resilience in this expansion, rejecting the bias of binary thinking.

⤞ THE BRIEF ⤝

We are two-sided, hybrid individuals with numerous dimensions and multiple desires, many of them contradictory. Paradox is woven into our nature and the fabric of life itself. Paradox isn't a problem, however. Our resistance to paradox causes suffering. When you adopt a dialectical way of seeing, as favored in Eastern cultures, opposition is simply what it is—neither good nor bad—making way for all your crooked parts. Waldo reminds us that we are spacious (an infinitude, in fact), with plenty of room for warring factions and vicissitudes. Entering this nondual realm, you're no longer threatened by your own strangeness; you recognize that the other is you. This awareness makes you bigger, not smaller; the tension of us-versus-them starts to loosen. You learn not to project your shadow onto others, and instead take responsibility for yourself with all your imperfections. You see that for every weakness, there is also a strength; that every darkness contains some light; and that each situation you meet, no matter how challenging, holds a potential for growth. You learn to turn the obstacle upside down by changing how you see, what you're attached to, using your imagination, and making new choices. This holism extends to flesh and spirit and the imaginary separation between your physical and metaphysical parts—which are indivisible. Realizing the oneness of experience heals the suffering of separateness and the judgment we feel toward our own contradictions.

On Resilience

Without Confidence, the Universe Is Against You

"Once you make a decision, the universe
conspires to make it happen."

The Cost of Living

We underestimate the impact of confidence on our ability to
flourish. *Confidence* derives from the same Latin root as *faith*
and rests on a foundation of trust in oneself and the willingness
to stand by our own decisions. Confidence is key to resilience as
well, and our capacity for holding our chosen course through life's
ups and downs.

Confidence comes at a humbling cost as well. Till you make
peace with your detours, disappointments, and backslides, you

cannot ground yourself spiritually. The truth empowers more than feel-good bromides, though, which simultaneously protect your ego while setting you up for a fall. Truthfulness girds us in times of challenge, and no progress is possible without failure, Waldo taught. Growth is gradual and incremental, marked by passages of near-invisible progress punctuated by sudden leaps forward. Without humility, we lack the necessary patience to build resilience. Waldo noted how grandiosity diminished the confidence of his peers, and he determined to lower his expectations. "I am thankful for small mercies," he admitted.

"[One] who expects everything of the universe . . . is disappointed when anything is less than the best," while one with more realistic goals is always "full of thanks for moderate goods" (*E*). Gratitude for all that we're given prevents us from lapsing into regret. Confidence is never helped by focusing on what we don't have or clinging to the past. Only by grounding yourself in *what is* do you increase resilience and self-assurance. "To finish the moment, to find the journey's end in every step of the road, to live the greatest number of good hours is wisdom," Waldo wrote (*E*). Self-reliance is learned by being fully present.

In Chicago, I meet a young woman named Adisa Krupalija who is a paragon of present moment awareness. An emigree from the former Yugoslavia, Adisa escaped the Balkan Wars with her family after weeks spent hiding in a basement. Eventually, the Krupalijas were airlifted to a Pakistani refugee camp before receiving asylum from the United States. Today, Adisa has a thriving career as an attorney and claims to be grateful for what the war gave her, despite having to leave her country.

"How did you do it?" I ask her.

Adisa smiles and sips her espresso. "I've always been independent," she says. "No matter what happens, I've always tried to focus on what I could learn from any given situation. Even in the camp, I was thinking, how can this improve me as a person? A lot of people were despondent, looking back at what they'd lost, but all I could think was, wow, I get to learn English! Now I get to see the world outside my little town."

I study her for signs of self-deception, whitewashing, but Adisa appears to be telling the truth. "You know, when you go through something like this, a part of you is changed forever."

"What part might that be?"

"It's the part of me that refused to conform. That can never be like other people. The part that's always pushing myself to be different, to take the harder path. To challenge myself to be stronger."

"That sounds like a lot of pressure for someone your age."

Adisa admits that it can be tiring. "But it winds up helping you a lot in the end. It gives you tenacity. An extra high tolerance for change and hard times."

Shaken from her comfort zone, she realized how malleable she actually was. Also, that life runs in cycles. Failure and loss trigger new beginnings. As Waldo writes, "Our life is an apprenticeship to the truth that around every circle another can be drawn." There is "no end in nature, but every end is a beginning." Our lives are circular as well, and their nature is to roll forward. "There is always another dawn risen on mid-noon, and under every deep, a lower deep opens," he tells us (*C*). Knowing that "another deep opens," that change is never-ending, and that mystery will carry the day inoculates us against fear of the unknown, providing confidence that we are equal to the worst. Psychologists call this *self-efficacy*, which is not quite the same as *self-esteem*. Self-esteem denotes the ability *to be* who we are happily inside our own skins. Self-efficacy points to the belief in our ability *to do* what we set out to do and actualize ourselves in the world. Self-efficacy leads to faith in our own endurance.

The researcher Albert Bandura established this distinction back in the 1970s. He was studying social cognition when he noticed a largely overlooked mechanism that plays a major role in human development. This mechanism was the individual's highly variable belief in her own ability to influence the events of her life. Bandura found that people with an "internal locus of control" tend to believe that what happens to them is greatly influenced by their own abilities, actions, and mistakes, whereas individuals with an "external locus of control" are inclined to imagine that outside forces, random chance, environmental factors, and the actions of others are primarily responsible for the events that occur in their lives.[1]

It's no surprise that folks with an internal locus of control experience far higher self-efficacy than those who believe they are puppets of fate. While self-belief alone does not ensure success, "self-disbelief assuredly spawns failure," Bandura found.[2] To complicate matters, people with low self-esteem can have unusually high levels of self-efficacy. Patricia Carew, a systems analyst in British Columbia, is such an anomaly. At sixty-one, Carew is the single mother of two adopted Chinese daughters, highly respected and successful in her field, and the kind of person you'd want on your team if you were stuck on a deserted island.

Carew also struggles with low self-esteem and a battered self-image that she is doing her best to strengthen in therapy. In truth, she's a study in opposites. Outwardly, she's a paragon of confidence and tenacity. Fiercely loyal and single-minded, Carew can make tough, unemotional decisions when necessary, doesn't take BS from anybody, and is markedly generous, kind, and warmhearted. Inwardly, she's highly self-critical and unforgiving of herself, unable to cut herself slack. "I can do anything for other people—go to the mat for the people I love," she tells me. "I'm a tiger mother with my daughters and make damn sure they get what they deserve." But her disconnect between self-efficacy and self-esteem can be hard to manage. "When it comes to doing things for myself, I find it next to impossible," Carew admits. "I'm doing my best to work on it but self-esteem is a bitch."

Confidence links to another quality that Waldo held in high regard: enthusiasm. Derived from the Greek for "filled with God," enthusiasm is a spiritual power that comes from being aligned with our purpose. As a young man, Waldo judged himself harshly for being insufficiently enthusiastic; he foundered on his lack of both self-esteem and self-efficacy. "All around me are industrious and will be loved, while I am indolent and shall be insignificant," he lamented in his journal.[3] He envied his friends their vitality and abandon. "Nothing great was ever achieved without enthusiasm," Waldo believed. "The way of life is wonderful [because] it is by abandonment" (*CIR*).

Waldo recognized that resilience and regret are counter-indicated. "Finish each day and be done with it," he told his daughters.[4] Acknowledging mistakes without shame, and taking the credit for what you do as well as the blame, fosters authentic confidence. Harnessing the locus of control within enables you to face setbacks with enthusiasm instead of self-pity. This builds balance and equanimity, Bandura concluded, increasing the ability to recover from failure. When success comes your way, you're happy to have it. When hardships arise, which they always do, you learn to view them as opportunities for self-compassion. This helps to guide you toward a win-win approach to life's uncertainties.

Confidence breeds new possibilities. "If the single man plants himself indomitably on his instincts, and there abides, the huge world will come around to him," Waldo promised (*TAS*). Intention magnetizes opportunities, relationships, and innovation. Scottish mountaineer W. H. Murray put it this way. "Until one is committed, there is hesitancy, the chance to draw back, always ineffectiveness," he wrote.

> [But] the moment one definitely commits oneself, the Providence moves too. . . . All sorts of things occur to help one that would never otherwise have occurred. A whole stream of events issues from the decision, raising in one's favor all manner of unforeseen incidents and meetings and material assistance, which no one would have dreamed could have come his way.[5]

Rumination leads to overthinking and endless inquiry into *why* things are as they are, which is often a complete waste of time.

Why Does Not Exist in Nature

Seeking definite answers to complex questions that can't be answered definitively is a fool's errand. While we must strive to understand our motives, ultimate causes can never be determined. We're subject to too many external variables in life; our certainties are hypotheses at best. Struggling to answer unanswerable questions robs a person of resilience because *why* does not exist in nature. The question why is a human construct that presupposes a logical universe where one plus one equals two and final outcomes can be predicted. There are no conclusive explanations for why things happen in the real world; reality is determined by a mysterious source whose workings transcend logic and reason.

To demonstrate that outcomes can never be predicted, the Stoics used the image of an archer. The archer does everything she can to shoot accurately, as Cicero famously observed. She strings her bow well, chooses her arrows with care, and studies the wind and the weather. Even so, she may miss the bull's-eye. No sooner has the arrow left her fingers than it falls outside the archer's control, subject to forces beyond her purview.[6]

Deciding upon a course of action, the wise Stoic carries it out to the best of her ability, knowing she cannot control the outcome. Thus subject to "externals" outside her control, she bases the success of her actions (as well as her self-worth) on how well she has prepared. In Seneca's words,

> The wise person considers intention, rather than outcome, in every situation. The beginnings are in our power;

the results are judged by fortune, to which I grant no
jurisdiction over myself. . . . Death at the hands of a robber
is not a condemnation.[7]

Accepting our limitations saves energy. Surrendering to the
unknown teaches us not to be victims; instead, we're agents of
change with limited options. With little knowledge of why we're
here, where we came from, or where we are going, we remain enig-
mas to ourselves. Waldo likens this existential quandary to finding yourself on a staircase with no idea of how you got there. "We
wake [at birth] and find ourselves on the stair," he wrote. "There
are stairs below us, which we seem to have ascended; there are
stairs above us, many a one, which go upward and out of sight"
(E). With birth comes a kind of amnesia, he tells us. Harking
back to Greek mythology, he suggested that each of us is over-
dosed on a memory-erasing elixir before we take birth.

> The Genius . . . which stands at the door by which we enter,
> and gives us Lethe to drink, that we may tell no tales,
> mixed the cut too strongly, and we cannot shake off the
> lethargy. Ghostlike we slide through nature, and should
> not know our place again. (E)

Is it any wonder that the question *why* is often so fruitless?
Nature never shows her cards completely nor fully reveals what
she has up her sleeve. When it comes to self-reliance, *how* is a better question than *why* on matters of personal growth. Behavioral
studies show that when we focus on *how*, we tend to be more

successful. "Goal orientation" is far more effective when it includes "implementation orientation." In one study, researchers tested a group of recovering addicts at a rehab clinic. The subjects were divided into two groups. The first group was asked to create a personal CV for employers before the end of the day. The second group was instructed to do the same while also including a plan of implementation. The differing success rates between the two groups was striking. While not a single subject in the first group completed a CV by the end of the day, 80 percent of the second group delivered their curriculum vitae on time.[8] Answering the question *how* provides traction and wherewithal for succeeding at tasks.

Life is in the doing, after all. An implementation orientation helps to overcome hesitation and self-doubt. Waldo pointed out:

> We are always on the brink of a notion of thought into which we do not swim. . . . Man postpones or remembers; he does not live in the present, but with reverted eye laments the past, or, heedless of the riches that surround him, stands on tiptoe to see the future. He cannot be happy and strong until he too lives with nature in the present, above time. (*SR*)

An internal locus of control prevents us from passing responsibility for our behavior onto our environment. We're no longer victims or helpless bystanders. Our lives are happening *through* us, not *to* us, we realize; seeking ultimate answers to *why* is futile. While blunders and absurdities no doubt creep in, tomorrow should be greeted as a new day, with a willing spirit, unencumbered by looking backward.

So take a moment to ask yourself: Do you tend to blame the world for your problems? Do you disempower yourself by shirking responsibility? Do you labor under the misconception that if you could only figure out *why* things happened, why you're the person you are, you'd finally gain control of your life? When we lose ourselves in such speculation, we become the playthings of circumstance.

Power and Circumstance

Waldo rejected the traditional notion of fate. Rather than seeing fate as part of a predetermined blueprint of a person's life, he viewed it as a composite of multiple factors. There's the time and place of one's birth, social station, intelligence, enthusiasm, charisma, and quality of choice making; most of all, fate is effectuated by an individual's responses to her conditions. "We have to consider two things, power and circumstance," Waldo suggested. Circumstance denotes the conditions one is given. "Nature is what you may do. There is much you may not" (*F*). Self-reliance demands that one acknowledge the facts, first. Magical thinking is counterproductive; fantasies of limitlessness or being saved by good luck do not help. He believed that "shallow men" believe in good luck, while "strong men believe in cause and effect." The "rough and surly" world will not "cosset or pamper us," Waldo reminds us (*F*); we're no more exempt from nature's laws than other animals. But we do have extraordinary powers of imagination and adaptation. "The water drowns ship and sailor like a grain of dust," he wrote. "But . . . learn to swim, trim your bark, and the wave which drowned it will be cloven by it and carry it like its own foam, a plume and a power" (*F*). Skillful navigation requires focused intention and humility before the overwhelming powers of nature. Such wise interaction determines our fate. "Forever wells up the impulse of choosing and acting in the soul," Waldo wrote. "*A part of Fate is the freedom of men* [my emphasis]. Intellect annuls Fate. So far as a man thinks, he is free" (*F*).

We must also allow for vulnerability. In Waldo's vision of self-reliance, vulnerability is inseparable from personal power. "Our strength grows out of our weaknesses. We acquire the strength we have overcome" (*CBW*). Fortitude increases in direct proportion to how much hardship we have known. Heroism is a universal trait, in fact, not the province of the elite few. He suggests that heroes aren't braver than the rest of us, necessarily. They're just "brave five minutes longer." This suggests a very different approach to strength than we're used to in macho America. A survivor of clinical depression told me much the same during an interview: "There are two ideas of bravery I like to play with," author Andrew Solomon said. "Is the brave person the one who rushes in and goes to the front line because he doesn't feel fear? Or is the brave person the one who is completely petrified but does something . . . not as much as the first person, perhaps, but done against the weight of their own fear?" Another voice of paradox after Waldo's own heart, researcher Brené Brown, elaborates on this paradox. "Vulnerability is not weakness," Brown makes clear, "and the uncertainty, risk, and emotional exposure we face every day are not optional."

> Our willingness to own and engage with our vulnerability determines the depth of our courage and the clarity of our purpose. The level to which we protect ourselves from being vulnerable is a measure of our disconnection.[9]

Vulnerability frees up the power we squander in attempting to appear fearless. This energy becomes available to us only when we let go of pride and ego—cease being "dwellers in a small hardness," as Waldo put it—and open to the divine inundation, the flood of life streaming around us.

⤙ THE BRIEF ⤚

Accepting your complexity builds confidence. Paradox is part of the cost of living. Humbled by life's challenges, you're made stronger by the knowledge that you are equipped to overcome adversity using skillful means. You learn to place the "locus of control" within yourself, rather than being a victim of circumstance, and to exercise the power of choice over how conditions impact you. Once you've achieved sufficient understanding of a situation, the question *why* becomes irrelevant, rarely guiding you where you need to go. *How* is far more beneficial when seeking inspiration, motivation, and resilience. Observing nature, you see this principle in action; nature is forever responding to conditions as they are, not backtracking to figure out how they became so. Similarly, when you grasp how much precious time and energy are wasted in retrospection, you learn to pay attention to what is present and doing the next necessary thing. Power and circumstance must both be factored in, knowing what you can change and what you can't, as you align yourself with larger forces.

On Vitality

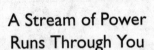

A Stream of Power
Runs Through You

"A man is a conductor of a whole stream of electricity."

Locating the Source

Waldo predicted that modern life would bring a disastrous disconnection from the natural world, as we've said, and a damaging loss of integrity and balance. "When human life in its guise as civilization ignores the laws of nature ... we fail and fall into chaos," he acknowledged. Yet the "broken giant" of humanity could yet "be invigorated by touching mother earth" (*H*). Echoing the Stoic belief that nature is the font of human virtue, he feared that distancing ourselves from the natural order would lead to our downfall. We "distrust and deny inwardly our sympathy with nature [and] . . . own and disown our relation to it by turns," he lamented (*N*).

When we divorce ourselves from Mother Earth, we sacrifice vitality and wholeness. Only by wedding ourselves to the organic creation do we regain our solidarity. This rapprochement rekindles our "raging desire for the whole" (*MON*); otherwise, we live "in division, in parts, in particles," separated from the "wise silence; the universal beauty, to which every part and particle is equally related." Recovering this sacred connection, we experience a world "whose beatitude is all accessible to us [and is] self-sufficing and perfect in every hour" (*O*). Such a homecoming quiets the clamoring mind that keeps us anxious and fragmented. "In the woods . . . I feel that nothing can befall me in life," Waldo wrote, "no disgrace, no calamity (leaving my eyes) which nature cannot repair" (*N*).

The healing power of nature can be startling in its impact. Nature reminds us that we belong (and are *whole*) in this divisive era of polarization. Dominique Mann, a writer who served in the Obama White House, learned this for herself as a child growing up in Sharon, Massachusetts, thirty miles south of the Old Manse in Concord.[1] A Black girl in a majority-white middle school, Mann spent years enduring racial violence and humiliation at the hands of classmates. To comfort herself, she took long walks in the woods with her mother, which helped restore her peace of mind. There was a special rock Mann would visit where she was able to "pause life" and ease "the pain of a world making me grow up too fast."

"Nature fortified my resilience as a biracial woman of color," she writes, bringing ease to her troubled mind "with each light whisk of the breeze, trickling creek, and rustle of wildlife." Today, Mann finds herself turning to nature with increasing frequency, especially since the murder of George Floyd and the explosion of the Black Lives Matter movement. Nature "promotes justice," she believes, and also helps with healing generational trauma, offering a "salve that feels almost instinctual." When the human-made world makes her feel invisible, nature grounds her, embracing her "as one of Her own."

"It felt like my humanity wasn't seen. But in the depths of lush forests . . . or amid the brown bears of Alaska, I knew the leaves wouldn't intentionally shrivel away from me; the breeze wouldn't decide I wasn't worthy," she has written. Nature became Dominique Mann's portal to higher consciousness, restoring her to her natural place in the universe.

As modern life becomes more virtual, the need to mend our relationship with nature increases in urgency. The temptation to lead conceptual, second hand lives must be resisted, Waldo teaches. To waste our inheritance is a tragic loss.

> Every rational creature has all nature for his dowry and estate. It is his, if he will. He may divest himself of it; he may creep into a corner, and abdicate his kingdom, as most men do, but he is entitled to the world by his constitution. (*N*)

Gratitude for our birthright enriches us. Assuming our rightful place in the web of creation engenders a sense of unity. "In proportion to the energy of his thought and will, he takes up the world unto himself," Waldo tells us (*B*).

This spiritual connection is linked to our biology. According to Andreas Weber, a German biologist and philosopher who pioneered the field of biopoetics, "Everything tends toward, or longs for, [this] connection."[2] According to biopoetics, living things can only be understood through the vitality they share with the rest of creation. All living things demonstrate the same "basic striving toward a deeper experience of oneself through another, which is the core of our aliveness." This principle pervades the natural world, according to Weber. "From the simplest cell to the most evolved human, the impulse to connect predominates," he writes. Life is, first and foremost, a "shared process of mutual transformation and productivity."

This principle of mutuality undergirds our existence. Creation takes place entirely within what Weber calls "poetic space"—which Waldo simply termed nature—and is shared by all beings. Unfortunately, the human-made opposition to nature prevalent since the Enlightenment threatens to bring this shared experience to an end. Such a split is not inevitable, however. Weber believes that a new "Enlivenment" is possible that can heal the false duality between ourselves and nature. He likens this potential transformation to the shift in modern physics that followed the discovery that an observer is entangled with whatever system is being observed. Such "entanglement happens emotionally and experientially through shared aliveness with other living subjects," Weber points out, bringing about a "deep change in our perception of reality." This perception illuminates the unity of all things regardless of how separate they might appear.

The World Is Not Two

Duality is a human-made phenomenon, as Waldo knew very well. There are no impermeable boundaries between phenomena in nature. What's more, nonduality (a central feature of the perennial philosophy) is an important aspect of self-reliance, though Waldo never used that phrase.

Nonduality reveals to us that all things in nature are indissolubly linked, that matter and spirit share the same source (as do humans and God), and that you and I, self and other, *are not two*. Despite the appearance of multiplicity and diversity, reality is one; every physical form emerges from the same ground of being. Things that appear to be opposites are antithetical in appearance only; fundamentally, they are forever joined. Like so many transcendental truths, nonduality seems to fly in the face of common sense. How can this desk I'm writing at be inseparable from the hand that's scribbling? How can wildly different forms be composed of the same formless substance, and how does this knowledge impact how we live?

Discoveries in quantum mechanics support the view shared by Waldo and mystics since the dawn of time, that the subatomic, invisible world is both unitary and in perpetual flux, formless and articulated in myriad forms.[3] Spiritually, our challenge is to remain aware of this unity while muddling through the diverse universe. As the Sufi poet Rumi suggested: "Live in the nowhere you come from even though you have an address here."[4] Fields such as quantum entanglement, dubbed Spooky Action at a Distance by Einstein, suggest that the tiniest particles are linked to one another even when separated by great distances.[5] The irrational notion that distant forms (including human beings) are communicating with one another in mysterious ways is a stretch for scientific materialists. Yet its implications for how we live are considerable. Waldo wrote,

> Man is a correlative of nature, whose power consists
> in the multitude of his affinities and the fact that his
> life is intertwined with the whole chain of organic and
> inorganic being. (N)

Details in nature, great and small, are universally bound together. "A leaf, a drop, a crystal, a moment of time, is related to the whole, and partakes of the perfection of the whole," he wrote (N). Acknowledging this unity wakes us up from the trance of duality wherein we appear to be separate from the world, trapped in the fiction of an autonomous self.

To understand how we're so easily deceived by appearances, it's necessary to consider how the illusion of duality is created. In its attempt to make sense of the world, the left hemisphere of the brain seeks difference and separation, creating categories where information can be bundled. This aspect of cognition isolates trees at the expense of seeing the forest. While this type of focus is for navigating through the material world, the division-happy side of the brain misses unity and interconnection, creating a semblance of reality based on imaginary boundaries and false separations. Waking up to nonduality threatens the ego's imagined sovereignty, however, which is why mysticism (transcendental consciousness in general) has never been widely popular. Luckily, science is finally calling our bluff by revealing the unity beyond the brain's dualities, and the need for a transpersonal (as well as personal) perspective in appreciating the holistic universe. Just as an alkaline battery requires two opposing terminals to ignite a single current, matter and spirit correspond to one another in similar ways, according to Waldo.

"The method of advance in nature is perpetual transformation," he reminds us (CON). Metamorphosis happens through the conjunction of opposites. Acknowledging nonduality dissolves mental barriers and fosters a spacious, more compassionate way of moving through our diversified world. We cease viewing ourselves as atomized subjects adrift in a universe of other separate beings; instead, we become part of a shared whole. When the ego's self-protective blindfold is removed, we perceive that our separate ("little me") self is less a discrete entity than a "selecting principle" intersecting with other selecting principles in an undivided universe.

"A rule of one art, or a law of one organization, holds true throughout nature," Waldo wrote (N). Unity awareness does not necessitate sacrificing our uniqueness or originality, however. Nature delights in variety—she wants you to be you and me to be me. As Waldo pointed out, individuality is not the problem; our hearts and minds are only impoverished when we forget the commonality underneath. This "lie of the mind" appears to divide us, though we're rendered from the same cosmic stuff. Waldo described the existence of "spherules," luminous bundles of energy moving at incredible speeds, "each one attracting or repulsing every other field in its region." Physicists describe these subatomic properties as quanta.

How does nondual awareness impact how we live? The potential benefits are impressive. Increasing our awareness of interconnection would strengthen our commitment to social justice, for starters. Recognizing ourselves as indivisible parts of a seamless whole could go a long way toward relieving our alienation as well. Nonduality could end our mistreatment of the planet, elevate our politics, counteract racism—tribal conflict in general—and accelerate our shift to integrative health care. A holistic view might well be the "remedy for all abuses," Waldo suggested. It is the cure for "all error in thought or practice . . . the conviction that underneath all appearances are certain eternal laws which we call the nature of things." An awareness that "the highest is present to the soul of man" might cure us of hopelessness as well, with the knowledge that

> the Supreme Being does not build up nature around us, but puts it forth through us, as the life of the tree puts forth new branches and leaves through the pores of the old. As a plant upon the earth, so a man rests upon the bosom of God; he is nourished by unfailing fountains, and draws, at his need, inexhaustible power. (N)

Learning from Nature

Nature offers surprising lessons in resilience, impermanence, balance, aliveness, struggle, and transformation. These instructions are central to the curriculum of self-reliance, far more vital than information we pick up in books. "What we do not call education is more than that which we call so," Waldo believed (*AOE*). God's preternatural tutelage through nature provides all we need to live an awakened life. "What is a farm but a mute gospel?" he asked (*N*). The farm teaches essential life lessons: to take only as much as we need, pay close attention to details, cultivate interconnection, and inhabit our spot on the planet with purpose and respect. "What noble emotions dilate the mortal as he enters into the counsels of the creation, and feels by knowledge the privilege to BE! . . . The beauty of nature shines in his own breast" (*N*).

Nature sometimes instructs us in mysterious ways. I had an experience years ago in a redwood forest that showed me how this teaching works. I was at a campsite near Crater Lake in Oregon with a soon-to-be-ex lover. We had a knock-down, drag-out fight that had left me furious and shaking. Before we started throwing punches, I walked away and found myself in a grove of towering redwoods that lined the path leading down to the lake. I was trapped in my thoughts, attacking this moron, and kept doing so as I walked this tree-lined path, ignoring the gargantuan trees around me. I kept going for a number of minutes, lost in my murderous fantasies, then I suddenly realized with genuine shock that my anger had disappeared—completely. No trace of it remained in my being. I knew intuitively that this grove of redwoods had healed my turbulent mind somehow, replacing rage with tranquility. Their ancient presence might have been whispering to me, "Forget this schmuck. Do we look worried?" Nothing of this kind had happened to me before (nor has it since), but this dose of "tree medicine" taught me a series of lessons I've never forgotten: that anger is shiftable, porous, and fleeting; that silence truly heals the mind; and that being in nature's company when you're down is better than Prozac, booze, or revenge.

Waldo puts this more eloquently. "The moral influence of nature upon every individual is that amount of truth which it illustrates to him," he writes.

> Who can estimate this? Who can guess how much firmness the sea-beaten rock has taught the fisherman? How much tranquility has been reflected to man from the azure sky, over whose unspotted deeps the winds forevermore drive flocks of stormy clouds, and leave no wrinkle or stain. How much industry and providence and affection we have caught from the pantomime of brutes. (*N*)

"Brutes" refers to those wordless creatures whose virtues are best appreciated through metaphor. Using anthropocentric sleight of hand, we learn to translate the encyclopedia of nature into human terms. "The instincts of the ant are very unimportant, considered as ants [but] the moment a ray of relation is seen to extend from it to man ... the little drudge is seen to be a monitor, a little body with a mighty heart" (*N*).

Nature's primary curriculum is silence. Language plasters labels on reality and interferes with direct experience. Spending time in nature deepens the unsayable; we grow more comfortable with the *unknowability* of things. Without the interference of language, the narrating mind is suspended; we're able to see in a new way. "When I behold a rich landscape, it is less to my purpose to recite correctly that order and superimposition of the strata than to know why all thought of multitude is lost in a tranquil sea of unity," he explained (*N*). In other words, it's possible to analyze a sunset, understand it meteorologically, chromatically, and miss the cosmic point of the experience. Waldo pushes us to deconstruct our alienation, understand when analysis blinds us, and transcend "this tyrannizing [tendency] in [our] constitution, which evermore separates and classifies things" (*N*). This transcendence allows access to our higher tier of emotions—wonder, awe, reverence, joy, delight, elevation, love—right brain faculties we will look at later. In her silence, nature trains us in wonder and awe, portals through which the mundane becomes miraculous.

Beyond the psychological helmet of self-centered worry exists a vast expanse where our "inner horizon extends miles farther," nature shows us. Expanded vision brings heightened awareness. Once again, "The health of the eye seems to demand a horizon [and we] are never tired, so long as we see far enough" (*N*).

We're also revivified by beauty. The soul needs beauty in order to thrive. Nature and beauty are inseparable, Waldo tells us. Beauty prompts gratitude and celebration, reminds us of life's miraculousness, and urges us to cherish our inheritance. "Is it not better to intimate our astonishment as we pass through this world, if it be only for a moment," Waldo wrote in his journal, "'ere we are swallowed up in the yeast of the abyss. I will lift up my hands and say Kosmos."

Kosmos was the Greek word denoting a particular kind of beauty, endowed with equal parts order and loveliness. When he encounters Kosmos, "a wild delight [runs] through the man, in spite of real sorrows" (*N*). Beauty shrinks pain down to its true proportion. That may be why the novelist Dostoyevsky believed that "beauty will save the world."[6] Without beauty, we forget who we are; numbness takes over, then self-pity, when we're cut off from its radiance. Waldo had no patience for the human tendency to wallow in pits of self-created despair. The dead zone of self-imposed exile from the sacred garden was of no interest to him.

In fact, his harshest judgments were reserved for complainers, ingrates, and pompous voyeurs, drowning in their solipsistic drama. "The misery of man appears like childish petulance, when we explore the steady and prodigal provision that has been made for his support and delight on this green ball which floats him through the heavens" (*N*). Rather than whine over our misfortunes, we're better served by learning perseverance, nimbleness, adaptation, generosity, simplicity, and endurance from nature. She teaches us through her terrestrial struggles that metamorphosis is ongoing, forms disappear, and the processes that govern human life are present throughout the whole of creation. Her example offers wisdom of biblical proportions.

From the first principle of growth in the eye of a leaf, to the tropical forest and antediluvian coal mine, every animal function from the sponge up to Hercules, shall hint or thunder to man the laws of right and wrong, and echo the Ten Commandments. (*N*)

We're able to recognize these commandments because we share in God's intelligence, the One Mind being expressed through individual awareness.

One Mind

People wedded to a dualistic view of existence imagine God (if they believe the divine exists) inhabiting a universe far, far away, overseeing our earthly lives from a vast, intergalactic distance. They reject the suggestion that the human mind partakes of the Mind of God and that individual intelligence is inseparable from its eternal source. How can their babbling, repetitive minds be iterations of divine Mind? they ask. Waldo came at this question the other way around. Where else do dualists imagine their intelligence comes from? "The river of thoughts . . . running out of the invisible world into the mind of men," he explained (*CFL*), proves beyond doubt that "there is one mind common to all individual men" (*H*).

The Stoics agreed. "What links one human being to all beings [is] not blood, or birth, but mind [since an] individual mind is God and of God," wrote Marcus Aurelius.[7] This does not imply that we control our thoughts; instead, like guests at a wayside inn, we observe the mind's comings and goings without knowing where its contents come from. Waldo reminds us that we are privy to this divine effluence but not its origins.

When I watch that flowing river, which, out of regions I see not, pours for a season its streams unto me, I see that I am a pensioner not a cause, but a surprised spectator of this ethereal water. . . . I desire and look up, and put myself in the attitude of reception but from some alien energy the visions come. (*O*)

This alien energy is transpersonal, issued by the universal Mind. Acknowledging the limits of our control, we cease feeling responsible for what we can't control. Over-responsibility is a key reason for our suffering, as Epictetus pointed out.

The chief task in life is simply this, to identify and separate matters so that I can say clearly to myself which are externals not under my control, and which have to do with the choices I actually control.[8]

We drop the painful fiction that we're masters of the universe and cooperate more intentionally with spiritual forces. We learn that "our painful labors are unnecessary and fruitless" (*SL*) and that "only in our easy, simple, spontaneous action are we strong." This relieves us of "a vast load of care" as well as attempts to "push the river" where we selfishly want it to go. Far better to

place yourself in the middle of the stream of power and wisdom which animates all who it floats and you are without effort impelled to truth, to right and perfect contentment. (*SL*)

Surrendering excessive control is necessary for creative growth. Every creator knows that when she's stumped with a project, it's far more effective to stop pushing, quiet down, and wait for an answer to "drop from the ceiling," as an artist friend says. When you stop trying to force the muse, and hit the pause button, you open yourself to the divine flow. You make way for genius and fresh inspiration to reach you from the mysterious source. Composer Igor Stravinsky did headstands to "clear the brain" when he found himself creatively blocked. Painter Salvador Dalí took "hypnogogic" naps to access the state between sleep and wakefulness when he lost artistic direction. Crime novelist Agatha Christie soaked in a hot bath eating fruit, apparently, whenever she got stuck in a book. There's a story about Steve Jobs, the founder of Apple, soaking his bare feet in toilet water, locked inside the company bathroom, when he needed to turn off the stress and tune in to the One Mind.[9]

Solitude is useful for this process as well, especially in the presence of nature. There, you discover that "the Highest dwells in [you] . . . that the sources of Nature are in [your] own mind," Waldo wrote (O). Extracting yourself from external noise amplifies the internal whisper. Reaching into your own deep currents, you touch the depths of the consciousness we all share, the reservoir of divine intelligence. This is where truth, beauty, and wisdom reside, in this timeless dimension. That's why poets, sages, and artists are able to speak to us across millennia, how their work stays relevant and relatable. You hear in their work echoes of what you already know. "In every work of genius, we recognize our own rejected thoughts. They come back to us with

a certain alienated majesty," Waldo wrote (*SR*). When you wel-
come "the influx of the Divine mind into [y]our mind," your
subjective thoughts merge with the "flowing surges of the sea of
life" (*O*), carrying you beyond yourself to the open expanse of
self-transcendence.

There, you meet the witness whose unfettered awareness links
you to the One Mind. Speaking sotto voce, the witness reminds
you that "within man is the soul of the whole" (*O*). We're encouraged to trust this inner prompting while rejecting outside
attempts to control our minds. Yet we often relinquish our mind-
states to others. Epictetus mocks us for this weakness.

> If a person gave away your body to some passerby you'd
> be furious. Yet you hand over your mind to anyone who
> comes along, so they may abuse you, leaving it disturbed
> and troubled—have you no shame in that?[10]

Waldo agreed with this criticism.

> It is easy in the world to live after the world's opinion. It
> is easy in solitude to live after our own; but the great man
> is he who in the midst of the crowd keeps with perfect
> sweetness the independence of solitude. (*SR*)

Paying humble, steady attention to your "upper dictation" clari-
fies the voice within. "Who shall define me as an individual? I behold with awe and delight the illustrations of the One Universal
Mind," Waldo noted in his journal.[11] No longer tethered by fear

and doubt, we learn to trust the spiritual consciousness we share
and its superior wisdom.

⊰ THE BRIEF ⊱

There is one power source in the universe. This life force,
known by many names, animates the entire cosmos, from the
aurora borealis to the houseplant on your windowsill. This
power exists inside you as well. By aligning yourself physically,
mentally, and spiritually with this transcendental power, you
experience unity with the world. You recognize dualism as a
human-made phenomenon and see that no such false separation exists in the eyes of God. Duality belongs to the realm of
appearances (the exterior life) that misleads you through your
senses. When you inquire into the nature of reality, you find
a single, indivisible current of being. Nature teaches you how
to stop, be silent, and experience this pulsing connection. She
teaches you patience and discernment as well. You recognize
the give-take, push-pull, expand-contract dynamic of reality,
so-called opposites comprising one dynamic whole. You share
the One Mind with all things that exist; this "higher dictation"
flows into you from mysterious ways, disappearing when you
least expect it. This intelligence holds unimaginable treasures
when you open your mind to the mysteries of the unknown.

On Courage

The Death of Fear

"Do the things you fear, and
the death of fear is certain."

Face Forward

Thirteen months after Ellen's death, Waldo's depression showed no signs of lifting. Unable to sleep, eat, or work, he brooded week after week in his study, oppressed by a grief he could not shake following the death of his beloved wife.

He was also mourning another loss, the death of his traditional Christian faith. Mortality had shaken his philosophical moorings. No longer able to administer the sacraments in good conscience, he found no spiritual succor in his ministry. The specter of death was too much with him. In the words of poet Mary Oliver, "Death's fast or slow lightning was a too-frequent presence"[1] in Waldo's life from the beginning, and now, after having watched Ellen waste away, his terror of leaving the world prematurely cast a pall on the life he'd been living. Waldo was scared of what lay ahead and needed a lifeline, desperately, an epiphany to lift him out of his darkness and throw off this shroud of morbid obsession.

On the frigid morning of March 29, 1832, Waldo left his home in Boston and set out in the direction of Mount Auburn Cemetery, having hatched a shocking plan to shake himself out of his paralyzing grief. He planned to open Ellen's coffin and confront her dead body with his own eyes. If he could face his worst fear, perhaps he could crack this ice floe of despair and move on with his life without her. I imagine Waldo as he looked that morning, making his way slowly on the snowy road, a gangly, handsome, slope-shouldered man with a mane of black hair and a craning, elongated neck. His ill-fitting overcoat barely covered his skinny legs; his ice-blue eyes were fixed on the ground, a fierce expression on his eagle-like face. He was probably familiar with the Buddhist practice of *maranasati*, in which monks and nuns practice meditation in charnel grounds, surrounded by skulls and skeletons, to overcome their fear of death. Hurrying toward the cemetery on that winter morning, Waldo aspired to do much the same with Ellen's corpse.

We'll never know what happened next, exactly. Waldo was atypically cryptic in his journal ("I visited Ellen's tomb today and opened the coffin"), but the results of this cemetery visit were obvious and life-changing. Within months, he'd resigned from his prestigious job at the Second Church of Boston, begun work on his first published book of essays, and set sail for a European tour. The liberation he experienced after his confrontation with Ellen's corpse left Waldo with surprising joie de vivre, the cosmic optimism that became his trademark. Despite his long life's numerous tragedies, he committed himself to never taking for granted "the unregarded epiphanies of every blessed day," according to his biographer Robert Richardson.[2]

Waldo came to believe with the Stoics that fear does a person more harm than the things of which she is afraid. Our responses to fear damage our overall health more than fearsome circumstances. The questioning of fear helps to loosen the grip of the fearmongering mind; conditions are rarely as catastrophic as imagination renders them. When we become sentries at the door of our own minds—like psychological bouncers—separating our allies from the gate-crashers, fear no longer hogs the dance floor. We're no longer behaving like wimpy hosts letting too many wild cards into the party. We learn to protect our minds from invasion, to neutralize fear through confrontation and understanding. Waldo taught that comprehension is our greatest weapon against terror. "Courage consists in equality to the problem before us" (COU). It is not that fear evaporates—poof!—but rather than being its prisoner, one assumes the role of interrogator. Scrutinizing the contents of fear builds courage. Fear doesn't disappear but our relationship to it is transformed. Making space for discomfort when it arises, allowing fear to be what it is, weakens fear's stranglehold on the mind.

This is a challenge we face every day: to freeze in anticipation of all the terrible things that might happen to us, or take a step forward despite our fears (as Andrew Solomon suggested). Crisis amplifies this necessity. Waldo was aware that nothing short of disaster on the scale of Ellen's death would have been sufficiently shattering to force him to reimagine his life, drop his role in the church, go rogue as an artist, and scrap the need for outside approval. When crisis strikes, it explodes expectations. You're no longer able to hide from the truth or distract yourself with mundane routines. The protective structures you've built to shield yourself from dangerous knowledge have been leveled. After your foundational structures crumble, leaving you exposed to the elements, you realize that ultimate safety was always a fiction. The less defended you are, the more lucid, open, and game you are likely to be. Mizuta Masahide, the seventeenth-century Japanese poet, expressed this in a haiku.

> Since my house burned down
> I now have a better view
> of the rising moon.[3]

We're meant to burn down our emotional houses on a regular basis, Waldo suggested, to enjoy the freedom left behind in the ashes. With a clear-eyed view of the challenges before us, we may find it within ourselves to prevail.

Equal to the Task

"Knowledge is the antidote to fear," Waldo tells us (*COU*). To the degree that you feel unprepared for or unequal to the task at hand, fear proliferates. He uses the example of a child struggling in class with his lessons to illustrate this point.

> A schoolboy is daunted before his tutor by a question of arithmetic, because he does not yet command the simple steps of the solution which the boy beside him has mastered. These once seen, he is as cool as Archimedes and cheerfully proceeds a step further. (*COU*)

Knowledge pushes the untutored child beyond his dread. Fear is highly personal, however, and can't be measured objectively. "The child is as much in danger from the staircase or the fire-grate, or the bathtub, or the cat, as the soldier from a cannon or ambush" (*COU*), in fact. Knowledge is the "encourager" that "takes fear out of the heart." We're as strong as we tell ourselves we are. ("They can conquer who believe they can.") Your unique composite of courage grows out of your particular character; it obtains from the combination of nature and nurture that singularly makes you yourself. This is an important point. "To be really strong, we must adhere to our own means [and not attempt to] adopt another's courage" (*COU*). No form of bravery is superior to another. "The courage of the tiger is one, and of the horse another." Nor is courage consistent across different contexts. We roar or whimper depending on conditions. "The dog that scorns to fight, will fight for his master," Waldo reminds us.

> The llama that will carry a load if you caress him, will refuse food and die if he is scourged. . . . There is a courage

of manners in private assemblies, and another in public assemblies; a courage which enables one man to speak masterly to a hostile company, whilst another man who can easily face a cannon's mouth dares not open his own. (*COU*)

A veteran firefighter named Michael Washington exemplifies this mixed bag of courage.[4] At six feet tall with a linebacker's frame, Michael is who you want breaking the door down to rescue you from a burning building. Before joining the fire department, he did four tours of duty in Iraq and Afghanistan in the Marines. As a full-time firefighter in a small California town, Michael proved himself a paragon of bravery in forest blazes, deadly mudslides, and other natural disasters; he was the picture of confidence in harsh situations. "We try to play that tough guy image as firefighters, law enforcement, military," he told an interviewer. Focused on those battles outside himself, he paid too little attention to the war within. He ignored the signs of PTSD, as well as memories of sexual abuse and other family violence. He'd compartmentalized his anxieties beneath a hero's mask; even when his son was killed in action in Afghanistan, he could not show his emotions at the funeral. Michael medicated his condition with alcohol and reckless behavior. "I needed to talk to someone," he said. "I was going down real fast."

It's fortunate that Michael's veteran buddies did an intervention. This led to therapy, becoming sober, and ceasing to take unnecessary risks with his life (he'd always been the first to volunteer for dangerous operations). After a grieving period of self-examination, he realized that he needed to share his story with other firefighters, to help keep them safe and encourage them to seek out help when they needed it.

Michael learned that bravery is not monolithic. He was terrified and heroic, powerful and helpless, vulnerable and mighty at the same time. We must not allow fear to have the last word; our power to rebound is surprising, even uncanny. Nature "made up her mind that what cannot defend itself cannot be defended," Waldo insisted. Also, that "God will not have his work made manifest by cowards" (*SR*). Aunt Mary had taught him well. "Always, always, always, always, always do what you are afraid to do," she encouraged her timid nephew.[5]

A healthy mind tolerates dangers without forgetting its own strength, acknowledges the monstrosities of human behavior without losing faith in its own resilience. Admitting the truth of evil inoculates us against dread and impotence, in fact. Even those "in whom every ray of humanity has been extinguished, parricides, matricides, and whatever moral monsters, do not disturb a healthy mind" (*COU*). Instead, we acquire a "patience as robust as the energy that attacks us." Miscreants and frightening creatures play a necessary role in the creation, Waldo insisted. "Wolf, snake, and crocodile are not inharmonious with Nature, but are made useful as checks, scavengers, and pioneers," he wrote. In other words,

> we must have a scope as large as Nature's to deal with beastlike men, detect what scullion function is assigned them, and foresee in the secular melioration of the planet how these will become necessary and die out. (*COU*)

Waldo's belief that destructiveness is part of the social fabric should not be misconstrued as complacency. He's not excusing bad behavior simply because it's "natural." Our task is to co-exist with evil without being destroyed by it, to remember that fear cannot defeat us when we approach it with open eyes. It also helps to acknowledge that the spectrum of human behavior exists within us as well, in its entirety. In the words of the Roman Stoic Horace, "Nothing human is foreign to me."[6] The knowledge that we also contain seeds of evil helps dissolve the barricade that exacerbates our fear of the other.

I saw a neighbor's life change after this realization following the attacks on 9/11. We lived a few blocks north of the World Trade Center and had watched together as ash-coated survivors trudged uptown past our apartment building on that terrible morning. This lovely woman had led a sheltered life of privilege and seemed devastated by the tragedy in a singular way. She wasn't bouncing back like the rest of us; terror seemed to have clamped down on her neck and wouldn't let go. She explained to me, clearly shaken, that death and evil seemed right next door for the first time. She'd never witnessed so much hatred, she told me in disbelief. Nor had she known—this was the kicker—that she herself was capable of wanting to murder. Having avoided this part of her shadow till then, she was ill equipped to deal with her fears. "I never knew I had it in me!" she said. It was the lack of knowledge about her own demons that was twisting her into knots of fear. For her, the ground rules of life had changed, leaving her in existential limbo. Had she taken the time before this (she was sixty-five) to explore herself, to learn what lay outside her cashmere bubble, she might have been more prepared for this present disaster, knowing human cruelty is nothing new.

Again, fear requires close scrutiny because we're so easily fooled by appearances.

> The eye is easily daunted. The drums, flags, shining helmets, beard, and moustache of the soldier have conquered you long before his sword or bayonet reaches you. (*COU*)

A frightened mind makes false assumptions based on incomplete information; it weaves narratives of terror to protect itself, using the imagination. Waldo noted that imagination is a potential liability when confronting fear, in fact. "Men with little imagination are less fearful," he believed. "They wait till they feel pain, whilst others of more sensibility anticipate it, and suffer in the fear of the pang more acutely than in the pang" (*COU*). Exaggerating danger weakens your resolve by convincing you that you are less capable than you actually are. The opposite of this tendency—macho bravado—brings a different set of dangers. "True courage is not ostentatious," Waldo wrote (*COU*), knowing that braggadocio can be lethal in extremis. His contemporary, Captain John Brown, was careful not to hire soldiers who pretended they were not afraid.

> As soon as I hear one of my men say, "Ah, let me only get my eye on such a man, I'll bring him down," I don't expect much in the fight from that talker. T'is the quiet, peaceable men, men of principle, that make the best soldiers.[7]

Secure in their battlefield knowledge, seasoned combatants neither downplay nor exaggerate peril. Rather than puff themselves up with bravado, they arm themselves with know-how, strategy, and skills to help temper their well-grounded fears.

Gauging danger realistically, we stand the best chance of success. When threats can't be gauged or are too overwhelming to reckon with, fear is likely to become chronic or unmanageable.

High Anxiety

Human existence has always been scary, but modern causes for anxiety and fear have multiplied a hundredfold since Waldo's day. In the grip of fear, societies regress, psychologically and spiritually. When reigns of "terror . . . madness and malignancy" are afoot, a "total perversion of opinion can take place . . . [that turns] society upside down," Waldo tells us (*COU*). Social science confirms that reactionary beliefs thrive in systems dominated by fear, making it easier for those in power to exploit the populace. Tolerance levels plummeted on a wide range of issues during the pandemic; on matters of immigration, sexual freedom, and racial equality, American policies regressed significantly.[8] The more afraid we are, the more primitive our attitudes become; liberalism shifts toward conservatism, independence to conformity, rehabilitation to punishment, openness to clan behavior, and personal choice to majority rule. The increase in hate crimes, gun violence, news-tampering, and reactionary law making—the general decline in civil liberties—offer definitive proof of the correlation between fear and social decline.[9]

There are hardwired, biological reasons why dangerous times point away from freedom. We're born with a kind of behavioral immune system that uses fear and conformity to help fight off danger, similarly to how the physical immune system creates antibodies to fight pathogens that invade the body. This behavioral immune system is our first line of defense against impulses that threaten our survival as groups and individuals. As some autoimmune disorders overstimulate the body's defense response and turn its protective mechanisms against itself, our behavioral immune system turns against us when social fears are on the rise. Trust of ourselves and others and the willingness to speak truth to power decrease as well when this system is activated.

Lene Aarøe, a Danish psychologist who studies the behavioral immune system, explains that such "better safe than sorry" logic may trigger preemptive fear reactions whether we are in danger or not, based on irrelevant stimuli.[10] These automatic responses often affect our decision making on issues that have nothing to do with the threat at hand. Since our early ancestors had no understanding of the specific threats that came their way, these overreactions are often crude and needlessly destructive. Aarøe explains that these "misinterpretations of irrelevant cues" happen when the "evolved mind" (the hardwired self-defensive brain) "meets the multiculturalism and ethnic diversity of modern times." We're left to negotiate the fears of our modern world with wiring installed in the Paleolithic.

As Waldo observed, "The smoothest curled courtier in the boudoirs of a palace has an animal nature, rude and aboriginal as a white bear" (N). These ursine responses are often preverbal, irrational, and primitive. They prompt what might be called pre-traumatic stress disorder—a debilitating dread of what's to come—which is what we're witnessing today. Over-vigilance, herd thinking, and the inability to transcend our gut responses all conspire against self-awareness and help drag society down to its lowest denominator.

With the behavioral immune system in high gear, we're manipulated more easily by unconscious fears, causing us to react in ways that make no sense whatever. In one study, Aarøe divided her control group in two; half the subjects were told to stand anywhere they wanted in the room where she'd placed them; the other half was instructed to stand next to a hand sanitizer. The results of this study were startling. The people located near the hand sanitizer expressed more bigoted, reactionary views than the group who chose their own places. The sanitizer-adjacent group became increasingly moralistic toward unconventional behaviors. Aarøe invited them to weigh in on a number of scenarios—having sex in your grandmother's bed, masturbating while holding a childhood teddy bear, even having dirty hands—and a majority of the sanitizer subjects turned in a punitive direction at the suggestion of such victimless crimes.

A century before psychologists invented a term to explain such reactions—"moral dumbfounding"—Waldo had warned that mistaking raw emotion for truth is hazardous to our mental health. Emotions are fickle and biased by nature, and our reflexive habit of holding indefensible moral judgments concerning things that *feel* wrong but cannot be proved to *be* wrong is an ethical trap. Moral dumbfounding undergirds racism, sexism, and senseless judgments that serve to increase our fears. Fortunately, when you realize how the behavioral immune system operates, you're better able to anticipate instantaneous, thoughtless judgments about people and situations. That's why it's imperative to question our knee-jerk reactions, which never account for the whole story. As Waldo observed,

> When a resolute young fellow steps up to the great bully, the world, and takes him boldly by the beard, he is often surprised it comes off in his hand, and that it was only tied on to scare away the timid adventurers.[11]

The power to unbeard our fears comes from mindfulness, challenging our overreactions to conditions that have no actual power to hurt us. Increasing knowledge not only helps us to grow; it also reduces fear and anxiety.

Fear of Freedom

Waldo himself was a poignant mixture of hero and coward, rebel and recluse; an advocate of nonconformity who was also a lifelong bourgeois rooted in his straitlaced habits. He acknowledged his own fear of freedom, coexistent with his desire for self-liberation.

> It is awful to look into the mind of man & see how free we are—to what frightful excesses our vices may run under the whited wall of [respectability]. Outside, among your fellows, among strangers, you must preserve

appearances,—a hundred things you cannot do; but inside,—this terrible freedom![12]

Fear of freedom is inherent to being human. French philosopher Jean-Paul Sartre described it as *la nausée*, the sickening awareness of how much choice we have in a vast, impersonal, chaotic universe. Psychoanalyst Wilhelm Reich explained it in this way:

> If we take freedom to mean first and foremost the responsibility of each individual to shape personal, occupational, and social existence in a rational way, then it can be said that there is no greater fear than the fear of . . . freedom.[13]

Trepidation in the face of our liberty can lead a person to think like a sheep; to define herself by her enclosures, and cling to the crutch of subservience.

Frederick Douglass was a fifty-five-year-old abolitionist and preacher when he first heard Waldo speak in Concord in spring 1844. Born into slavery, Douglass, whose father was white, had escaped from the shipyard in Baltimore where he was indentured, smuggled himself into Pennsylvania, changed his name, gotten married, obtained a preacher's license, and lived as a free man. On the day he listened to Waldo speak about the spiritual lives of formerly enslaved Blacks—in particular, Waldo's use of the term *anti-slave*—Douglass realized that his drive toward external freedom had failed to unlock his internal shackles. Waldo spoke of the psychological emancipation necessary for Blacks in America and the need to confront their fear of freedom if they hoped to emerge as anti-slaves. Without the force of character necessary to seek and maintain their free state, they would forever remain slaves, he told them in an 1844 lecture, "The Emancipation of the Negroes in the British West Indies."

Douglass took this challenge to heart and later responded on its impact. He shouldered the "severe cross" of truth "reluctantly" and accepted the veracity of Waldo's message. "The truth was, I felt myself a slave," Douglass wrote, "and the idea of speaking to white people weighed me down." He would eventually make this shift to become an anti-slave, which came as a kind of resurrection.

> My long-crushed spirit rose, cowardice departed, bold defiance took its place; and I now resolved that, however long I might remain a slave in form, the day had passed forever when I would be a slave in fact. I did not hesitate to let it be known to me, that the white man who expected to succeed in whipping, must also succeed in killing me.[14]

It's wrong to compare the experiences of slaves to the challenges faced by the rest of us. Yet it is also incontestably true that every individual must seize her own freedom, if she is to maintain it. That means dropping self-denigrating beliefs and building awareness that no one else can control her. As Americans, this resistance to freedom can be hard to spot, concealed by the popular belief in our unshakable national privilege. Still, underneath the belief in our inalienable rights, we remain indentured in ways that escape our attention, spiritually and intellectually, lulled into passivity by material comforts. Waldo warned against such entrancement, the willingness to persuade ourselves that we're free when we're simply locked inside a cushier cage. We must not mistake the glitter of stuff with the gold of self-reliance, he tells us. This means acknowledging the ways in which we are hemmed in, shame-ridden, and cowardly, how we fear our own power and allowing our voices to be heard. Waldo knew that vulnerability can be scary and that there is no terror like that of being known. Intimacy may be a threshold to freedom, but it's not always easy to cross, especially when it comes to love and allowing others into our hearts.

❧ THE BRIEF ❧

Fear is exacerbated by avoidance and denial; it is alleviated by close attention to the things that cause you the most discomfort. Fear proliferates in the dark, which is why it must be exposed to the light of attention. When you inquire into the source of your fear, two things happen; first, the fear itself is diminished; second, you often discover that the actual source of your fear is not what you believed it to be. When you're specific about your fears and the stories surrounding them, and assess the difficult conditions themselves, you equip yourself with knowledge, which is the strongest antidote to fear. You realize that you are equal to the challenge—that you are bigger than your fear. This endows you with courage, which is not the same as fearlessness. Fearlessness isn't the absence of fear; it's the capacity for fear to exist without it stopping you. Bravery is a subjective virtue measured by how much insecurity, vulnerability, and resistance have been overcome when you're afraid. Living in a time of maximal fear, barraged daily by dystopian news and threats to personal and planetary survival, vigilance toward fear is critical lest it cripple or dominate you. Pay careful attention to your negativity bias and the tendency to indulge your fears and dire predictions, which can easily fulfill themselves; also, pay attention to your fear of personal freedom and the responsibilities it brings. This includes whether or not to open your heart in love, to expose yourself intimately to other people, which can be the scariest decision of all.

On Intimacy

Love Is the Masterpiece of Nature

"The love that you withhold is the pain that you carry."

A Thorn in the Flesh

Waldo's tragic flaw was his terror of emotional intimacy. He craved close connection and pushed it away, torn between his standoffish nature and the Stradivarius of his intense emotions. He burned inwardly with passion while upbraiding himself for his chronic froideur. As he complained in his journal, "I have not the kind affections of a pigeon."[1]

Still, he rhapsodized over love's supremacy in his writing. "The sweet sincerity of joy and peace which I draw from this alliance with my brother's soul is the nut itself whereof all nature and all thought is but the husk and the shell," he wrote in his essay on friendship. Friends sometimes mistook his aloofness for a lack of feeling, but that was far from the truth. Bronson Alcott, his neighbor in Concord, once likened Waldo to "an eye more than a heart, an intellect more than a soul."[2] Another neighbor reportedly compared seeing him in the street to meeting a man on stilts. These criticisms were far off the mark. In truth, Waldo was as easily overstimulated, intellectually and romantically, as a mooning teenager struggling to appear grown up to the world.

This contradiction created an emotional gap between himself and other people. Sadly, this sometimes included his own family at times. "Most of the persons whom I see in my house I see across a gulf," Waldo confessed. "I cannot go to them nor them come to me."[3] This estrangement could be agonizing for him. "Strange is it that I can go back to no part of my youth, no past relation, without shrinking and shrinking," he reported in his journal. It pained Waldo terribly to know that those dearest to him ("not Ellen, not Edward, not Charles") had never known him completely. "If [my brothers] could have read my entire heart"—rather than his staid exterior—"they should have seen . . . generosity conquering the superficial coldness and prudence." He lamented that he wasn't "made like these beatified mates of mine, *superficially* generous and noble, as well as *internally* so. This is the thorn in the flesh."[4]

This emotional wound fueled Waldo's life as a writer, seeker, and philosopher, however. Had he not been such a failure in love, his drive to plumb the mysteries of the heart might never have been so extensive. The "pilgrim's progress" each person makes in his life is driven by necessity, after all. However difficult intimacy was for him, Waldo never doubted love's value as the summum bonum of human existence. Heartbreak and love were fused in his psyche, starting with his mother's benign neglect. Ruth Emerson—widowed, beleaguered, withdrawn—doled out affection like castor oil (only when needed), which did little to satisfy her sensitive middle son. The void where his mother's love should have been, deepened by his father's and brothers' deaths, never filled in Waldo's lifetime.

Still, he could extract sweetness from this bitter fruit like a master vintner allergic to the grape. The intoxication of intimacy left him sick—he became punch-drunk too easily on far too little, suffering miserably the morning after. Yet Waldo longed to drink deep. More than erotic love, he craved soul-stirring conversation with peers, spiritual meetings of the heart and mind, however rare they proved to be.

> Sincerity is a luxury allowed, like diadems and authority, only to the highest rank. Every man alone is sincere [but] at the entrance of the second person, hypocrisy begins. (*FR*)

Waldo's sensitivity to duplicity was so extreme because he found insincerity so painful. Love cannot be authentic, he knew, without an equal measure of truth.

Truth and Tenderness

Friendship was the ideal container for love and affection between two people, he believed. "[The] private and tender relation of one to one . . . is the enchantment of human life" (*L*). Intimacy must include a meeting of minds to be truly satisfying. Waldo grew impatient with the banalities of mundane conversation and could be intolerant of petty vanities. For this reason, he was often ill at ease with people, sometimes laughing or snickering at embarrassing moments. He criticized harshly and often overdid his praise.

Intellectual affinity must be present for love to flourish, Waldo believed, whether the relationship is platonic, romantic, or something in between. Beautiful as Ellen Tucker was, his love for her would not have been so intense had she not been an aesthete and poet as well. His second marriage, to Lidian, was relatively successful because she, too, was solitary and contemplative. Though Lidian longed for their "modulated expression of love" to blossom into an authentic intimacy, this was not to be.[5] In his journal, Waldo described theirs as a "Mezentian marriage," alluding to the Roman myth of the cruel King Mezentius, known for tying men face-to-face with corpses and leaving them to die.[6] Poor Lidian didn't stand a chance.

Waldo believed that two elements are essential to all forms of love: truth and tenderness. Relationships can only thrive when both parties are true to themselves, first and foremost. One should never place her desire for love above her own integrity. Each person must "guard [their] strangeness," he wrote (M), as "truth is handsomer than the affectation of love" (SR). A true friend must "not cease an instant to be himself" (FR). Far better to be "a nettle in the side of your friend, than his echo."

> The condition which high friendship demands is ability
> to do without it. . . . Let it be an alliance of two large,
> formidable natures, mutually beheld . . . before yet they

recognize the deep identity which beneath these disparities unites them. (*FR*)

It's imperative to respect the inviolate space that exists between even the most intimate loved ones. Individuals are "globes which can touch only in a point," he believed (*E*). Czech poet Rainer Maria Rilke echoed this insight when he compared true lovers to "two solitudes that protect, border, and salute one another." Rilke elaborated: "A merging of two people is an impossibility, and where it seems to exist, it is a hemming-in, a mutual consent that robs one party or both parties of their fullest freedom and development.

> But once the realization is accepted that even between the closest people infinite distances exist, a marvelous living side-by-side can grow up for them, if they succeed in loving the expanse between them, which gives them the possibility of always seeing each other as a whole and before an immense sky.[7]

Waldo the introvert marveled that different cosmic bodies could intersect at all across such vast psychological expanses. Human isolation is only bridged by *attention*, he insisted, and such attention gives rise to a "sort of paradox in nature" (*FR*) capable of remedying existential loneliness.

> I who alone am, I who see nothing in nature whose existence I can affirm with equal evidence to my own, behold now the

semblance of my being in all its height, variety, and curiosity, reiterated in a foreign form; so that a friend may well be reckoned the masterpiece of nature. (*FR*)

Intimacy requires concerted effort as well, beginning with a tolerance of our loved ones' flaws. As Waldo knew from experience, the most cherished, compatible person is bound to disappoint you sooner or later. Even in the "golden hour of friendship," he noted, "we are surprised with shades of suspicion and unbelief" (*FR*). Relationships fluctuate like all things in nature. "The systole and the diastole of the heart are not without their analogy in the ebb and flow of love" (*C*). Authentic connections require candor and directness. "I do not wish to treat my friends daintily, but with the roughest courage," he claimed (*FR*), though Waldo wasn't always able to live up to this challenge himself. Also, deep bonds are not forged overnight; they require time and commitment, like all organic processes. The laws of love are "austere and eternal . . . one web with the laws of nature and morals" (*FR*). We often forget this in the social media age, when friendship appears to be only a mouse click away, and intimacy on demand seems guaranteed. We aim at "a swift and petty benefit," Waldo complained (*FR*) and fail to take the time for love to mature.

Maturation happens through dialogue—deep talk—which is the "practice and consummation" of love. Interior worlds are bridged with language, he believed. Friends who explore deep talk together have a chance of being uplifted, inspired, transformed by meaningful conversation. Turning their attention to matters of importance, they form a kind of spiritual triangle whose vertex is transcendence. Such relationships are rare, but when they happen, people discover their best self; in deep conversation, a "tacit reference [is] made to a third party, to a common nature" (*O*), which embodies both people. This presence is bigger than the individuals; "it is impersonal; is God," Waldo tells us. People engaged in meaningful conversation

> become aware that the thought rises to an equal level in all bosoms. They all have a spiritual property in what was said, as well as the sayer. They all become wiser than they were. It arches over them like a temple, this unity of thought in which every heart beats with nobler sense of power and duty.... All are conscious of attaining to a higher self-possession. It shines for all. (*O*)

Intimacy is not always high-minded, of course. Waldo could be mischievous and silly with family and friends. "It is one of the blessings of old friends that you can afford to be stupid with them."[8] Elsewhere, he wrote, "If you do not quit the high chair, and roll on the ground a good deal, you become nervous and heavy-hearted."[9] Still, he longed for those deeper connections that eluded him and left him lonely, disappointed that Providence "will not give me what I want, in the shape of a man or a woman."[10]

An exception to this rule was Margaret Fuller, who met the Emersons through a mutual friend in 1836. Seven years Waldo's junior, Margaret was widely considered to be the most learned woman in New England. Her spiritual love affair with Waldo was arguably the most intimate and complicated of his life, and a godsend to them both while it lasted. Margaret was the first person in Waldo's life who refused to respect his rigid boundaries; her trespasses, irritating and aggressive as they could be, forced him to tolerate emotional messiness in ways that were new to him and provided—in addition to frequent discomfort—a great deal of joy.

Mesmerized by Margaret's brilliance, and thrilled by her company, Waldo was utterly immune to her feminine charms, which wounded and frustrated her.* Margaret had fallen in love with Waldo both spiritually and sexually, despite his being a married man. As a gender-fluid renegade born a century before her time, Margaret was a thoroughly modern woman who enjoyed the risk and ambiguity of their relationship. In an era when friendships between married men and unmarried women were taboo, Margaret's dangerous liaison with Waldo pushed the bounds of social decorum. Flattered by Margaret's attention, Waldo invited her to join the Transcendental Club and to edit its literary review, *The Dial*. He waxed lyrical in their correspondence, in language befitting a lovesick fool. "O divine mermaid or fisher of man, to whom all gods have given the witch-hazel wand . . . I am yours & yours shall be," he wrote in a letter.[11] His ardor quickly drained away when Margaret was in the room, though. His rejections left Margaret to wander around Waldo's library, stroking the spines of his books.

Still, the sentimental education he received through Margaret

---

* In addition to having a nasal voice and a nervous habit of incessantly opening and shutting her eyelids, Margaret was corpulent and had an unsightly skin condition. She compensated for a curved spine by walking with her head thrust forward, "like a bird of prey," and, from her schooldays on, was "the kind of obnoxious know it all—brusque, sarcastic, and self-important—who invites mockery." (Judith Thurman, "The Desires of Margaret Fuller," *The New Yorker*, April 1, 2013)

was invaluable to Waldo, teaching him that tolerating unruly, threatening feelings is part of the price of intimacy. Waldo learned how much he needed this emotional wrecking ball in order to bring down his defenses. "A mind might ponder its thought for an epoch and not gain so much self-knowledge as the passion of love shall teach in a day," he noted (*H*). His conflicted feelings for Margaret could not be grokked with common sense. He cherished their "strange, cold-warm, attractive-repelling conversations" while acknowledging his ambivalence toward a woman "who I always admire, most revere when I nearest see, and sometimes love,—yet whom I freeze, and who freezes me to silence, when we come nearest."[12]

Eventually, Margaret's aggressive advances forced Waldo to step away from their close relationship. She could not control her feelings, though she tried. "This darting motion, this restless flame shall yet be attempered and subdued," she promised, but was unsuccessful.[13] Eventually, Waldo thanked her for her refusal to respect his extreme self-protection. "I shall never go quite back to my old Arctic habits," he promised Margaret in a letter, and his respectful love for her never wavered.[14] After Margaret was killed in a shipwreck a few hundred yards off the New York coast at the age of forty, along with her Italian husband and baby boy, Waldo paid tribute to her genius and originality in his eulogy. "She bound in the belt of her sympathy and friendship all whom I know and love," he remembered. "Her heart, which few knew, was as great as her mind, which all know."[15] Problematic as their friendship was, its pith—the core of love at its center—remained intact despite their personal issues.

Love Isn't Personal

The culmination of love is self-transcendence, Waldo came to see. Love and self-centeredness are mutually exclusive. When it comes to "the holiness of the heart's affections," John Keats's poetic phrase, form is less important than content.[16] His affection for Margaret remained identical in its essence although the shape of their friendship changed.

At its core, love is timeless, formless, agenda-free, simple, regenerative, and bound up with nature. The impersonal power of love helps us weather the trials of intimacy without closing our hearts under pressure. Recognizing love's metaphysical status infuses our imperfect unions with spirit. Conflicts become opportunities for humility, openness, and insight. Waldo advises us to look at relationship as a spiritual practice, viewing our beloveds as souls-in-progress. Doing so reveals the part of one's being that *is* love, the spirit that is never diminished by hardship and shines through in the act of giving.

Love is not personal, in other words. What's more, love is not a feeling, although its expression can be pleasurable. Relationships prompt different emotions and sensations, but the spirit behind these responses is the same. The self-cherishing ego rejects this idea, which seems to contradict its *specialness*; yet, it's true that love is formless in essence while manifesting differently in different conditions. As gravity supports all heavenly bodies, love sustains human bodies in orbit. Certain spiritual traditions, including Zoroastrianism, suggest that gravity and love are one and the same; that the power propelling the galaxy through space is identical to the one driving human attraction. As travelers through this mysterious realm, we are "put in training for a love which knows not sex, nor person, nor partiality," Waldo tells us (L). Love fulfills its true purpose when it pushes us past our personal limits, bridges the false separation between self and other, and communes with the spirit underneath. He likens this communion to a conflagration.

> For it is a fire that, kindling its first embers in the narrow nook of the private bosom, caught from a wandering spark out of another heart, glows and enlarges until it warms and beams upon multitudes of men and women, upon the universal heart of all, and so lights up the whole world and all nature with its generous flames. (L)

Spiritual love exceeds the sum of its parts. It pushes us beyond our assumptions and attachments to convention. Lovers rediscover the affinity that initially drew them together and learn to separate the false from the true; as the window dressing of relationship falls away, the spiritual design underneath is revealed. Waldo uses the example of newlyweds to make this point. As love matures, husband and wife come to see that "those once sacred features, that magical play of charms" that most enchanted them "was deciduous . . . like the scaffolding by which the house was built" (L). They realize that "the purification of the intellect and the heart from year to year is the real marriage, foreseen and prepared from the first, and wholly above their consciousness." This echoes Plotinus's belief that "Love refines and purifies the soul."[17] As trust builds, we grow capable of generosity *that does not depend on reciprocation*. We become plentiful and free enough to share the love moving through us without keeping score.

> Why should I cumber myself with regrets that the receiver is not capacious? It never troubles the sun that some of its rays fall wide and vain into ungrateful space, and only a small part on the reflecting planet. (*FR*)

Instead, we allow "[our] greatness [to] educate the crude and cold companion." We learn that love is not an object to be coveted but a radiance emanating from our core. Love is no longer viewed as a commodity to be measured or lost or exchanged as you'd barter a trophy or prize. Free of its possessive, competitive disguises, love becomes a gift that can only be shared when it's free. While "it is thought a disgrace to love unrequited, the great will see that true love cannot be unrequited," Waldo wrote (*FR*). When we love in the way that God might love, fearing neither rejection nor pain, we shift from transaction to transcendence in our approach to intimate relationships.

I learned this for myself after a miserable breakup. I'd been dumped by the dreaded individual with whom I was camping in Oregon. I was oscillating between outrage and sadness, but another emotion was present as well: intense pain over having lost something *in myself*—my faith in love, perhaps, or at least belief in my own ability to love. I wasn't sorry to end this relationship; what I regretted was feeling that I had been damaged, as if a part of my heart had been stolen, the aspect that was willing to be vulnerable and open.

A few weeks after the breakup, feeling especially out of my mind, I left my apartment and wandered aimlessly around the city, trapped in the bedlam of my own thoughts. Finally too exhausted to walk any farther, I found a bench on a quiet side street. Closing my eyes, I could feel the sun on my face, and when I opened my eyes a few minutes later, I realized what a gorgeous day it was. The heat felt fantastic on my skin, a crystalline sky was draped overhead, a gentle breeze began to blow, and the scent of jasmine was wafting toward me. Soon I felt my darkness lifting, with the startling beauty of the world before me. I heard myself say out loud, "I can't live this way anymore." Two questions suddenly appeared in my mind. What is the actual source of your sadness? And has your ability to love actually been taken from you? With this second question, an insight struck me. I saw clearly that my heart was intact although I was feeling a lot of pain; I was still a loving person, and no one could stop me from opening my heart. I was free to love without holding back, and nobody could stop me. I could love anyone as much as I wanted (including my ex) and did not need their permission. I sensed the knot in my solar plexus opening up, and I started to feel like myself again. I was not the victim here, and no one could smother my desire to love. This felt like a great restoration of power. Although it was twenty years ago, this realization that love isn't personal has never left me, and it even helps sometimes when relationships get rocky.

Love reminds us of the interconnection that belies our surface differences, Waldo taught. This web of love is supported by selfless intention more than by heated emotion. This fosters an intimacy with the world that personal attachment and projection preclude. We realize the degree to which we shield our hearts out of fear of this ubiquitous intimacy, and how self-protection leads to insensitivity. The Stoics taught that *sympatheia*, "the affinity of parts to the organic whole," is a portal to self-realization. *Sympatheia* is the artery of interconnection that gives access to our full humanity. "The universe made rational creatures for the sake of each other," Marcus Aurelius wrote, "with an eye toward mutual benefit based on true value and never for harm." Elsewhere, he added, "What is bad for the hive is bad for the bee."[18] Love modulates greed and disinterest, isolation and egotism. The illusion is dissolved that our personal welfare is separate from the welfare of others.

> Every being in nature has its existence so connected with other beings that if set apart from them it would instantly perish. Insulate a man and you annihilate him. He cannot unfold, he cannot live without a world. (*H*)

Isolation is solitude deprived of self-love; that's why isolation impoverishes and solitude enriches the spirit. Isolation is loneliness-adjacent. Research shows that loneliness leads to declines in cognitive function, prosocial behavior, motivation, and longevity. The shadow of individualism is loneliness, which opens a chasm between oneself and others. Unfortunately, our competitive culture gives us very mixed messages about *sympatheia*. In the harsh climate of American meritocracy, dependency is too often seen as weakness. Compassion is denounced as evidence of a "nanny state," an excuse to coddle people who exploit the system. A faction of conservatives harbor deep skepticism toward too much public love; interdependence—as a principle on which to base public policy—is highly suspect.

Whether we're speaking of personal relationships or the social contract, exaggerated fears of dependency are anathema to love. Generosity and vulnerability are both given short shrift. It takes a strong person to ask for help, however, and to trust that she is supported by others. The humility needed to express personal needs actually increases self-reliance. Fear and hubris obscure *sympatheia*. The heart remains cramped in its bud till we allow ourselves to open to kindness. "Emotions of benevolence . . . from the highest degree of passionate love, to the lowest degree of good will . . . make the sweetness of love," he reminds us (*FR*). An invisible current of fellow-feeling surges through our shared existence. "We have a great deal more kindness than is ever spoken" (*FR*). The chill of reticence fails to freeze love in its dynamic path. "Barring the selfishness that chills like east winds the world," he wrote, "the whole human family is bathed in an element of love like a fine ether."

> How many persons we meet in houses, whom we scarcely speak to whom yet we honor, and who honor us! How many we see in the street, or sit with in church, whom, though silently, we warmly rejoice to be with! Read the language of these wandering eyebeams. The heart knoweth. (*FR*)

Relationships change, affections alter, grief comes and goes, but the filament binding humanity together remains as strong as ever. We touch one another in that open space beyond personality, pride, and fear. "Out beyond ideas of wrongdoing and rightdoing there is a field. I'll meet you there," Rumi promised. This transpersonal field is Waldo's destination as well. We are here to witness and love one another during our brief time here on earth. Especially when times are hard, intimacy is a path of salvation.

THE BRIEF

Love is the summum bonum of existence. It is also among life's greatest challenges. The inability to love is a "thorn in the flesh"; it confirms the ego's fear that it is alone and unlovable. We cut through this fake news with truth and tenderness, indispensable engines of intimacy regardless of the type of relationship. Honest communication is vital—when we relate to each other as souls, companions on the path of awakening. When we recognize love's spiritual nature, human connection is elevated, even sanctified. You realize that love isn't personal, that the love you feel for a parent, friend, or lover is the same love (as your mind is an iteration of the One Mind), rendered from the same sweetness. Though unconditional love may be out of reach, transpersonal love is always possible. You learn to transcend human surfaces, touch peoples' essence, recognize the other in yourself (and vice versa). This is a difficult, immensely rewarding process of learning to recognize God in all things. It's imperative to remember "inter-being," resisting the urge to self-isolate, especially in times of pain. We're supported, nurtured, and energized by others, which is also why it's imperative to be vigilant about the quality of the company you keep.

On Adversity

When It Is Dark Enough, You Can See the Stars

"Bad times have a scientific value . . .

the good learner would not miss."

The House of Pain

Waldo viewed hardship as nature's corrective, an opportunity to transform pain into insight. He was as unsentimental as the original Stoics about accepting life's inevitable losses. Adversity can endow you with second sight, he taught, the aptitude to detect growth potential when all seems lost. As the poet Theodore Roethke wrote, "In a dark time the eye begins to see."[1]

When you shift your angle of vision and silence your negative predictions, misfortune can guide you to higher ground and surprising outcomes. Waldo offered no fuzzy blanket of consolation but a tough-love recipe for freedom instead. When we recognize that hardship can have an ulterior purpose, we're better prepared to meet grief and pain.

> The death of a dear friend, wife, brother, lover, which seemed nothing but privation, somewhat later assumes the aspect of a guide or genius, for it commonly operates revolutions in our way of life, terminates an epoch of infancy or of youth which was wanting to be closed. (*C*)

Crisis shakes up the status quo, as I've mentioned. Leaving "a wonted [habitual] occupation, or household, or style of living" allows for the establishing of "new ones more friendly to the growth of character" (*C*). After all, when it comes to the universal cycle of birth, death, and transformation, we can only influence the final stage. We can choose whether to be enlarged or diminished by impermanence; pain can be used to isolate ourselves in self-pity, to justify our obsession with the past, or as an opportunity to connect with other suffering beings. We can't mature without knowing loss. "He has seen but half the universe who has never been shown the House of Pain," after all (*TT*).

No theory of life can be valid that does not include the suffering inherent to our condition. Without acknowledging the value of "vice, pain, disease, poverty, insecurity, disunion, fear, and death," Waldo argued (*TT*), we miss essential lessons. "Nature is upheld by antagonism," after all. "Passions, resistance, danger, are educators. We acquire the strength we have overcome" (*CONS*).

Rather than become embittered by life's disappointments, it's wise to lower our expectations and prepare for plenty more. Marcus Aurelius advises us to begin every day with this sobering exercise. "When you wake up in the morning, tell yourself: The people I deal with today will be meddling, ungrateful, arrogant, dishonest, jealous, and surly."[2] Prepared for the worst, whatever pleasantness crosses your path will come as a delightful surprise. You've learned that seeking lasting satisfaction from people and things that are bound to change and ultimately disappear is a terrible mistake. It is far wiser to ground ourselves in spirit, which absorbs and sustains all manner of trouble, without losing its lightness. "The spirit is true to itself," he wrote,

> and learns to live in what is called calamity, as easily as in what is called felicity, as the frailest glass-bell will support a weight of a thousand pounds of water at the bottom of a river or sea bed, if filled with the same. (*TT*)

The element that buoys us is spirit, without which life's trials are likely to crush us. Without the transcendental, we're too weighed down by the materialist view. We risk condemning ourselves to a pessimistic outlook masquerading as realism (a point we explore further in the next lesson). However, "The furnaces of affliction suddenly become fountains of living water, all springing from humanity," poet William Blake assured us, when we allow this transformation to happen.[3] Waldo elaborates: "If [people] have the degree of *buoyancy* and resistance that makes light of these mishaps the scars rapidly cicatrize and the fiber is all the tougher for the wound" (*F*).

Lack of spiritual awareness makes it harder to find creative solutions when the chips are down. That is why the law of compensation rubs materialists the wrong way. People immune to spirituality tend to resist the idea that adversity can have an upside. Materialism leads to pessimism and a tendency to revel in unhappiness, Waldo warned, which puts you at a severe disadvantage when life throws you curveballs. "Tragedy . . . consist[s] in temperament, not in events," he made clear. Certain people have "an appetite for grief."

> Pleasure is not strong enough and they crave pain. . . .
> No prosperity can soothe their ragged and disheveled
> desolation. They mis-hear and mis-behold, they suspect
> and dread. They handle every nettle and ivy in the hedge,
> and tread on every snake in the meadow. (*TT*)

Transcendentalism helps you transform the snakes in the meadow into helpmeets, advisers, and sages. Otherwise, you remain trapped on the surface of things, and the "exterior life" makes us unhappy. Melancholy belongs to the exterior life, and anti-spiritualists cling there as long as possible. Eventually, adversity makes it impossible to hold that illusion together, as Waldo wrote:

> Whilst a man is not grounded in the divine life by his
> proper roots, he clings by some tendrils of affection to
> society. But let any shock take place . . . any revolution . . .
> and at once his type of permanence is shaken. (*TT*)

Loss leaves no stain on the spirit, however. When you acknowledge the relative unimportance of material change, wounds become more bearable, he suggests. Waldo came to this realization unexpectedly after Wallie's death. Despite the enormity of his loss, he was startled to find that a part of him had remained untouched; that nothing essential had been taken from his interior life. Waldo's spirit was intact though his heart was split open. He explored this paradox in his journal:

> So it is with this calamity. It does not touch me:
> something which I fancied was a part of me, which
> could not be torn away without tearing me, nor enlarged
> without enriching me, falls off from me, and leaves no
> scar. (*E*)

How is this possible, we ask ourselves? To understand this paradox, it's necessary to make a clear distinction between emotional and spiritual reality. One belongs to the exterior life while spirit characterizes the interior dimension where love doesn't die and nothing is lost, though cherished forms change shape. It's not that exterior losses don't matter, but they matter far less than we believe they do. Waldo mused over this distinction. "The only thing that grief has taught me, is to know how shallow it is." Even Wallie's death,

> like all the rest plays about the surface, and never
> introduces me into the reality, for contact with which,
> we would even pay the costly price of sons and lovers. (*E*)

What does he mean by this? Simply that our spiritual nature, which is loving and good, is even more precious to us than our passing emotional connections. The emotional ear may hear this as callous, but the spirit knows that Waldo is speaking the truth. His equanimity did not reflect a flaw in his fatherly love. Instead, it was a truthful confession of spiritual awakening after terrible loss. "In the death of my son . . . I seem to have lost a beautiful estate,—no more," he wrote in amazement. "I cannot get it nearer to me" (*E*).

When you understand that grief is not monolithic, immovable, or unchanging, that you process experience differently in diverse parts of yourself, you're not as disturbed by complex responses to loss. After my best friend died six years ago, I was surprised by my polymorphous reaction. We'd shared the most important phases of our life for decades. We had been each other's wingman through multiple storms. After an unexpected cancer diagnosis, he died in three months. While Robert was dying and afterward, I was aware of an absence of some conventional feelings I would have expected to experience in this sad time. Though I miss Robert every day, my sadness over his death has never touched my love for him. I was at peace when he passed. Robert had lived a rich and meaningful life. He'd loved and been loved, excelled in his field, traveled the world, explored himself deeply. While I wish he were here to gossip with, a less selfish part of me is unbereaved. My gratitude for forty years of happy memories far exceeds my bitterness over time we've lost. Waldo's cherished memories of his beloved Wallie far outshone his despair and continued to inspire him throughout his life (his last words were, reportedly, "that beautiful boy"). Though his heart was broken, he had no regrets.

Waldo believed that hearts are made to be broken, as the saying goes, and *that* is why God sends sorrow into the world.

Thankfulness for things as they are, including the parts we'd never have chosen, is foundational to self-reliance.

Include All Things in Your Gratitude

Waldo teaches us that it is possible to bear loss and pain with thankfulness rather than resentment. Self-reliance does not ask us to suppress our true feelings or whitewash our grief. He prescribed gratitude as an antidote to despair, holding the transcendental view alongside our emotional life. This frees us from solipsism and bitterness. The Ojibwa people of North America have a prayer that reminds them of their true place in the world. "Sometimes I go about in pity for myself and all the while a great wind carries me across the sky," they say. Hardship is part of the human inheritance we have been prepared to shoulder. Another prayer from Sufism puts this beautifully.

> Overcome any bitterness that may have come because you were not up to the magnitude of the pain that was entrusted to you. Like the mother of the world who carries the pain of the world in her heart, each of us is part of her heart and is, therefore, endowed with a certain measure of cosmic pain. You are sharing in the totality of that pain. You are called upon to meet it in joy instead of self-pity.

The prospect of meeting misfortune with joy may ring woo-woo to a materialist. But pain, no matter how intense, belongs to the exterior life and can't harm you in a lasting way unless you cling to the past, Waldo made clear. "All loss, all pain, is particular; the universe remains to the heart unhurt" (*SL*). Emotions are akin to weather and leave no mark on the open sky. Yet we often confuse feelings for meaning and purpose and lose ourselves in emotional extremes. Drama gives a jolt of aliveness.

> There are moods in which we court suffering, in the hope that here, at least, we shall find reality, sharp peaks and edges of truth. But it turns out to be scene-painting and counterfeit. (*E*)

When you see your pain for what it is, the past no longer controls you, and the myth that suffering brings significance can finally be cast aside.

Waldo and the Stoics emphasized that we have dominion over how we carry our past. We are free to frame our memories as we please, to enrich our lives or diminish them. We have the ability to place different stresses on life events and remember the beauty of what we lost. As Seneca said, "If you admit to having derived great pleasures, your duty is not to complain about what has been taken away but to be thankful for what you have been given."[4] When you lose yourself in lamentation, you risk stripping away the delights of the past, the beauty of those memories. You can obscure love's afterglow with pain. Never-ending grief is an insult to the memory of our beloveds when we forget the rest. "Has it then been for nothing that you have had such a friend?" Seneca asked.

> During so many years . . . after such intimate communion of personal interests, has nothing been accomplished? Do you bury friendship along with the friend? Believe me, a great part of those we have loved, though chance has removed their persons, still abides with us. The past is ours, and there is nothing more secure for us than that which has been.[5]

How can Seneca be suggesting that the past, of all things, is *secure*? By reminding us that the choice over how you view the past rests with you, what you decide to make of your memories. You alone have the power to redeem your losses through gratitude and giving back. No one can prevent you from being thankful for the life you have lived with its "ten thousand joys and ten thousand sorrows."

The psychological and physical benefits of gratitude are well known. Gratitude raises levels of dopamine and serotonin, neurotransmitters responsible for our emotions, and fortifies the neural pathways that lead to wellness. Gratitude has been shown to improve brain functions and prompt a long-term decrease in toxic emotions.[6] These statistics hold true whether an individual has expressed her thankful feelings to others or not. One study of a thousand teenagers concluded that those who kept a gratitude journal reported a remarkable increase in generosity and far less focus on materialism. What's more, the control group that kept a gratitude journal donated 60 percent or more of their earnings to charitable organizations than non-journal keepers.[7] Cicero called gratitude "the parent of all human feelings" because it leads to the desire to care for others.[8] Gratitude makes it easier to not lose sight of our blessings or be blinded by pain when bad things happen, knowing they're not the end of the story.

After the Ruin, the Resurrection Is Sure

The spiritual practice of wise remembering stops us from being trapped in the wreckage of the past. We see that renewal after destruction is a natural process. "I am defeated all the time, yet to victory I am born," Waldo wrote in his journal.[9] Our "temper and elasticity" are part of our wiring. "How fast we forget that blow that threatened to cripple us," he reminds us (*TT*). "Nature will not sit still," after all. "New hopes spring, new affections twine, and the broken is whole again" (*TT*).

For such regeneration to occur, we must be open to the possibility. A photographer named John Dugdale was given a crash course in resurrection after suffering a series of devastating losses. Following his AIDS diagnosis in 1988, John lived through three major strokes, five bouts of pneumonia, toxoplasmosis, peripheral neuropathy, Kaposi's sarcoma, and CMV retinitis that left him nearly blind. In his Greenwich Village apartment, he tells me, "Losing my eyesight at the beginning of my career was the thing I dreaded most of all." John is a strikingly handsome, square-jawed man with a perfect nose and a crown of dark hair, recalling a portrait by John Singer Sargent.

"Everyone told me that my career was over," John says. "But I decided that if I was going to lose my eyesight, I wanted to do it in a courageous way, hanging onto my camera tripod not strung up to an IV pole."

Hospitalized for seven months, John decided that if he survived, he would become the world's first blind photographer. "Vision and sight are not the same thing," he explains. "Survival doesn't really mean anything without acceptance. That's the paradoxical part." John reaches down to pet his seeing-eye Lab. "You have to take the thing that's wrong and own it. You have to make it into something that has meaning for you. If you try to hide or negate it, it will just eat you up. If you're hoping for things to be other than they are—constantly wondering how or *why* something happened, or how to fix it—you're lost."

The opportunity for transformation when we enter deeply into our experience is absolutely unbridled, John learned. "It's like nuclear power if you choose to use it properly. But if you can't imagine yourself in a new way, you're just not gonna make it. If you think you're going to be the person you were before tragedy struck—internally or externally—it's impossible. Once you pass through that fire, you've been smelted. You're gonna come out gold on the other side or you're not going to come out at all." Proving his doctors wrong, John has had over forty solo shows internationally since being told his photography career was over. "And my best work is yet to come," he believes.

Humility is an integral part of this resurrection process. As Waldo put it, "A great man is always willing to be little." Such a person is also willing to endure discomfort, knowing it can make him bigger. "Whilst he sits on the cushion of advantages, he goes to sleep," wrote Waldo. "When he is pushed, tormented, defeated, he has the chance to learn something" (*C*). After Wallie died, Waldo received a condolence letter from an admirer who was worried about his mental state. He thanked her for her concern but assured this kind lady that his head and heart were quite intact since "the powers of the soul are commensurate to its needs."[10] Tragedy does not require that we become slaves of our past or forget the power of nature to heal us.

There's a time to grieve and a time to let go. Languishing too long in regret can inhibit your powers of recuperation. It's present-moment awareness that builds resilience, meeting the day with beginner's mind. Waldo instructs us to find the journey's end in every step of the road and to remember that living "the greatest number of good hours" is wisdom. In Waldo's view, "five minutes of to-day are worth as much as five minutes in the next millennium" (*E*). Your power exists only in "the moment of transition from a past to a new state, in the shooting of the gulf, in the darting to an aim" (*SR*).

It's often hard to know in times of struggle whether you are healing or not. That is why patience and trust in dark times are key to recovering from devastation. "In times when we [think] ourselves indolent, we have afterwards discovered that much was accomplished and much was begun in us," Waldo wrote (*E*). Anyone who's lived through a life-changing crisis knows how difficult it is to know whether she's making progress or not. Mysterious forces work through us, reorganizing our inner worlds, preparing us to meet our new normal. Studies in post-traumatic growth confirm that uncertain times are ripe for transformation. Psychologists describe the "positive disintegration" that can take place after major loss, explaining that the potential for personal growth is multiplied when we "explore our own thoughts and feelings surrounding the event."[11] Cognitive exploration prompts curiosity and increases our ability to find personal meaning in adversity.

Reflection leads you out of the woods; the world regains its loveliness. We remember ourselves as children of God. "When we look at ourselves in the light of thought, we discover that our life is embosomed in beauty," after all (*SL*). The shroud falls off the present moment, and pain loses its morbid attraction.

> Behind us, as we go, all things assume pleasing forms, as clouds do far off. Not only things familiar and stale, but even the tragic and terrible, are comely, as they take their place in the pictures of memory. (*SL*)

Even in our darkest hours we see that "it is only the finite that has wrought and suffered [and that] the infinite lies stretched in smiling repose" (*SL*). If we could secure ourselves in this knowledge, we might come to realize the futility of regret, knowing that

> there is no need of struggles, convulsions, and despairs, of the wringing of hands and the gnashing of teeth, and that we miscreate our own evils. (*SL*)

In the end, the refusal to move past our pain "interfere[s] with the optimism of nature," he tells us (*SL*). This prevents us from reentering the forward stream of life with all its powers of renewal and invention.

THE BRIEF

There is no wholeness without an acquaintance with suffering. A person must have tasted grief, loss, disappointment, distress—the dark side of life—if she hopes to develop true compassion and a tolerance for impermanence. When entering the "house of pain," it's crucial to take a good look around and notice the cracks where the light gets in and to remember that character is formed (and made formidable) by the hard things one overcomes. Gratitude is the antidote to self-pity. Cultivating an attitude of thankfulness (gladness) for the experience of being alive, learning to bless the details of life using the practice of *amor fati* (love of fate), even when they are unpleasant, helps a person grow in spiritual stature and deepen her connection to the God within. She surrenders to the cycles of life, including periods of misfortune, knowing they're leading to "secret destinations of which the traveler is unaware." Creation and destruction are knitted together; after things fall apart, they reemerge in new forms, rising from the ruins of what has been lost. Resurrection is wired into our nature. Deaths of all kinds are necessary for new growth and flourishing to take place.

On Optimism

The Soul Refuses Limits

*"Don't waste yourself in rejection,
nor bark against the bad, but chant
the beauty of the good."*

Lightening Up

The religious dogma of human evil was enjoying a heyday in Waldo's era. New Englanders, descended from Puritan stock, were suspicious of claims of human goodness (and happiness in general) as respectable goals for ordinary people. Penance, self-mortification, and pious judgment were the preferred moral coins of the realm. Waldo was tutored in pessimism and shame, a worldview in which human beings were seen as fallen creatures, tattooed with sin from the time of our birth, carnal fleshpots bound for hell.

He loathed this pessimistic view and attributed it partly to ancestral melancholy among British settlers, linked to hereditary depression. "The Tragic cleaves to the English mind in both hemispheres as closely as to the strings of an Aeolian harp," wrote Waldo, who kept just such an ancient instrument in his own study (*TT*). Pessimism is the enemy of faith, he believed, a boulder in the path of human potential. Goodness lies dormant in even the most reprobate individuals, he insisted. In a world composed of light and shadow, our nature is to *brighten*, to journey from ignorance to self-knowledge. "Even in the mud and scum of things, something always, always sings," he wrote in a poem.[1] "The measure of mental health is the disposition to find good everywhere" (*NHI*). Goodness, beauty, and truth have the power to guide us from the shadows of pessimism and self-condemnation when we learn to listen to our higher angels.

Waldo challenged the pessimism of cynics who refuse ideas that threaten to dispel their gloom. "Don't waste yourself in rejection, or bark against the bad, but chant the beauty of the good," he suggested (*S*). The problem, he knew, is that pessimists often defend their negativity by calling themselves realists. The pretense of objectivity is pessimism's great conceit—it's con job, you could say—the bogus suggestion that the more hopeless you are, the more realistic you must be. Waldo refused this ersatz realism and its negative, anti-imagination, evil-obsessed ethos. He maintained that if pessimists would devote more time and energy to examining their self-fulfilling prophecies, and focus less on attacking optimists, human life would improve dramatically.

It is arrogant to assume the worst, he tells us. There are too many variables beyond our ken. How can anyone with a passing awareness of life's mysteries *not* be struck by their limited knowledge, he wondered, humbled by all that is unknown to them? Pessimism marks a failure of the imagination, in fact, a deadly betrayal (and underestimation of) the human spirit. He recognized that the materialist view is our greatest ethical albatross. In one Hindu parable with which Waldo may have been familiar, materialists are likened to a colony of frogs that inhabit the bottom of a dark well. The frog majority believe that their dank, narrow dwelling represents the whole of reality, but one courageous frog is not convinced. When this rebel can no longer suppress her curiosity, she climbs out of the well, hops to the edge of a cliff, and finds a vast, glittering ocean as far as her bulging eyes can see. When the "enlightened" frog returns to tell the others what she's discovered, none of her slimy cohorts believe her. This is similar to how pessimists treat optimists who attempt to tell them the good news. Information that threatens the consensus view is relegated to the ideological fringe.

This was Waldo's dilemma, as a rebel who had glimpsed the sea and wanted nothing more than to spread the good word to a culture suspicious of transcendental wisdom. His contemporary, educator John Dewey, described the effect of Waldo's message on those who were ready to hear it. "His coming was like the sun breaking through the clouds for people long living under dreary skies," Dewey wrote. He'd "taken away the barriers that shut out the sun" for a swath of Americans hungry for the light.[2] There were many who mocked Waldo's optimism, preferring their own abysmal weather over his pie-in-the-sky predictions. Novelist

Herman Melville was one such naysayer who admired Waldo personally but held his hopeful view of humankind in contempt. Melville, along with fellow writer Nathaniel Hawthorne,* founded the Anti-Transcendentalist group, whose mission was to argue against what they viewed as dangerous spiritual vacuity among Waldo and his peers. Anti-Transcendentalists maintained that selfishness, evil, greed, and hatred were the sine qua non of human nature. They put their faith in Old Testament misanthropy and accused Waldo of ignoring the problem of evil and humanity's darkest impulses.

They were grievously mistaken. Cosmic optimism does not downplay evil; Waldo was as gimlet-eyed about human destructiveness as anybody in New England. But he also believed that good is infinitely more powerful than evil and that we must not define evildoers by their worst mistakes. Except for sociopaths with severe mental illness, sinners were rarely beyond rehabilitation. Like the ancient Stoics, he viewed evil against a spiritual background. This "ground of being" is never harmed even as we do serious damage to one another. "Nothing is evil which is according to nature," Marcus Aurelius wrote, adding that "the existence of evil does not harm the world."[3] The Anti-Transcendentalists believed this was hogwash. Of course evil is inexcusable and must

---

* "I had heard of him as full of transcendentalism, myths & oracular gibberish," Melville noted. "To my surprise, I found him quite intelligible. . . . I love all men who dive. Any fish can swim near the surface, but it takes a great whale to go down stairs five miles or more," Melville reported (in Michael McLoughlin, *Dead Letters to the New World* [New York: Routledge, 2015], p. 85). What's more, there is a direct line of materialist thinking leading from the Anti-Transcendentalists to Richard Dawkins's *The Selfish Gene* and certain of the New Atheists of our time.

be punished appropriately, Waldo and the Stoics agreed. Yet evil passes like everything else. Being impermanent and part of the exterior life, its importance must be acknowledged but not exaggerated. "Evil is merely privative not absolute. It is like cold, which is [merely] the privation of heat," Waldo pointed out (*DSA*).

He was well aware of how unpopular these transcendentalist ideas were in the mainstream, however, knowing that devotees of the exterior life believe only in what they can see, hear, touch, taste, or smell. Though idealistic, Waldo was never a fantasist. His godson William James, the renowned psychologist, explained this in a memorial talk he gave twenty years after Waldo's death. "[The] conviction that Divinity is everywhere may easily make of one an optimist of the sentimental type that refuse[s] to speak ill of anything," James explained, but "Emerson's drastic perception of differences kept him at the opposite pole from this weakness." He went on to clarify that "his optimism had nothing in common with that indiscriminate hurrahing for the Universe with which Walt Whitman has made us familiar." Instead, Waldo's genius lay in his ability to acknowledge evil without condemning flawed human beings, James told the audience, his ability to view evil contextually as emerging from negative life conditions. He made it clear that

> to know just which thing does act in this way, and which thing fails to make the true connection, is the secret . . . of seership. Emerson was a real seer. He could perceive the full squalor of the individual fact, but he could also see the transfiguration.[4]

This ability to hold contradictory views simultaneously is the very definition of wisdom, as we've learned. The capacity to bridge paradox makes it possible to be both hopeful and realistic.

The Substance of Hope

A historian named Kate Bowler learned this lesson about genuine hope versus fatuous optimism after a life-threatening crisis.[5] Kate was the mother of a one-year-old child, married to her high school sweetheart, and happy in her academic career, when, at thirty-five, she received a diagnosis of stage 4 stomach cancer and instructions from her doctor to go home and settle her affairs. It seemed cruelly ironic that Kate had recently written a book called *Blessed*, tracing the history of the Prosperity Gospel, a homegrown American philosophy of positive thinking that gained popularity in the 1960s. According to the Prosperity Gospel, God rewards us when we do the "right things" and possess the "right kind of faith." As Kate explains, "If you're good and faithful, God will give you health and wealth and boundless happiness in life. The gospel served me well until it didn't."

Realizing that the Prosperity Gospel had failed her, she recognized the need to look more deeply into her own beliefs about optimism. "I had to face the fact that my life is built with paper walls and so is everybody else's," Kate says. After going public about her situation in a *New York Times* op-ed, she found herself barraged by letters from readers assuring her that her cancer had happened "for a reason," that it was somehow "part of God's plan," but Kate had begun to see it differently, as she describes in a popular TED

Talk. "What I've learned in living with stage 4 cancer is that there is no easy correlation between how hard I try and the length of life," she told the audience.

She has been surprised by unexpected insights as well. "When I was sure that I was going to die, I didn't feel angry, I felt loved. It was one of the most surreal things I've experienced. At a time when I should have felt abandoned by God, I was not reduced to ashes." Instead, Kate discovered that her own ordeal had bonded her more profoundly with others in pain. "It was a feeling of being more connected somehow with other people experiencing the same situation." This left her with a less willful, outcome-oriented, transactional view of what constitutes prosperity. "I see that the world is jolted by events that are wonderful and terrible, gorgeous and tragic," she continued. "The one kind of Prosperity Gospel that I believe in [is that] in the darkness, even there, there will be beauty and there will be love and every now and then it will feel like more than enough."[6]

Waldo emphasized that "informed hope"—as opposed to magical thinking—is good for emotional and spiritual health. In William James's own pioneering work, fueled by ongoing struggles with physical illness and suicidal depression, he pointed out that optimism has been necessary to our species' survival. "The human mind and emotions are not made for this pessimistic philosophy and cannot live in sanity and health with it," James wrote. While our sphere of influence may be small, and we're subject to forces we can't control, reminding ourselves that we have a few choices at our disposal—including the choice to help—"keep[s] the iron bands from pinching beyond endurance."[7]

Cynicism is the enemy of hope, as pervasive today as it was in

Waldo's time. Disillusionment has been a perennial problem in a country founded on vaunting ideals, where injustice, corruption, and social inequity are rampant, nonetheless. "Americans have many virtues, but they have Faith or Hope," he lamented. "I know no two words whose meaning is more lost sight of" (*MTR*). Waldo attributed this spiritual shallowness to braggadocio and self-congratulation. "Our America has a bad name for superficialness," he noted. "Great men, great nations, have not been boasters and buffoons, but perceivers of the terrors of life, and have manned themselves to face it" (*F*). We must leaven overweening pride with humility, gird our optimism with self-knowledge, and avoid the trap of hubris.

Hope and gratitude are central to the constellation of emotions linked to optimism. Like gratitude, hope emphasizes the goodness that already exists rather than focusing on positive qualities that are missing. Hope increases psychological and physical fitness in observable ways. Research shows that belief and expectation, key elements of hope, are known to block physical pain by releasing neuropeptides in the brain that mimic the effects of morphine. Both expectation and belief assist the nervous system and increase select hormones that improve outcomes.[8] In order for hope to have a healing effect, though, it must take obstacles into account. Physician-author Jerome Groopman describes the difference between helpful and harmful forms of hope gleaned from decades of clinical practice. "False hope can lead to intemperate choices and flawed decision making," Groopman writes. "True hope takes into account the real threats that exist and seeks to navigate the best path around them."[9]

The value of realistic hope is illustrated by what's come to be known as the Stockdale Paradox.[10] James Stockdale, a POW during the Vietnam War, discovered a method for maintaining hope against insurmountable odds that was not based on denial. The Stockdale Paradox states that it is possible to maintain strong faith that we can prevail while simultaneously confronting the most brutal facts of our current reality. Informed optimism keeps hope's door open, warming us with possibility in our coldest hours. Such hope is not very different from faith, though it's not based on theology. It's faith in the power of life itself to heal, reconfigure, begin again. This faith is like the one Rabindranath Tagore, the Bengali poet, likens to a "bird that feels the light and sings while the dawn is still dark."[11] The capacity for song in darkened times is the essence of optimism. Spiritual awareness helps you transcend the appearance of impossibility, which pessimists take to be the bottom line, and remain open to positive change.

We're born with an optimism bias as well as a negativity bias, it's important to remember. The optimism and negativity biases both serve our fitness for survival. While the better-known negativity bias keeps us alive in dangerous environments, the optimism bias has allowed us to survive impossible situations by imagining alternate realities. "This bias protects and inspires us," in the words of one researcher. "It keeps us moving forward, rather than to the nearest high-rise ledge."[12] In a fluctuating environment, we must be able to imagine positive outcomes if we hope for transformation. In the 1960s, the flower children's optimistic vision of love grew directly out of their hatred for the Vietnam War. Assaulted by My Lai's horrors and assassinated American heroes, the hippies responded with a passionate plea to somehow get ourselves back to the garden.

It's hard to be a pessimist in the presence of spring's awakening. To free ourselves from the devil's bargain, we must return to the innocence of the natural world and secure our faith and optimism. The Reverend Martin Luther King Jr., among America's greatest Transcendentalists (the "arc of the universe" bending toward justice could have been Waldo's credo), pleaded with us to step off the "hamster wheel of earning and spending," in Waldo's words, and remember our sacred connection to life. "Somewhere along the way we have allowed the means by which we live to outdistance the ends for which we live," King preached.[13] He knew that affluent societies that fail in this task, losing perspective on the *means* through which they're prospering, sacrifice their communal soul.

Despite his discontent with America's direction, Waldo fully believed that his generation was superior to those that had preceded it, and he remained hopeful that future generations would surpass their forebears. This progressiveness gives Waldo's teaching its distinctly American flavor. We are heirs to a flourishing universe, he maintained, and hope is our human birthright.

The Moral Sentiment

Waldo described the "moral sentiment" as that faculty of goodness that "never forfeits its supremacy," even if it cannot always be felt. This moral sentiment is coeval with the "secret, sweet, and overpowering beauty [that] appears to man when his heart and mind open to the sentiment of virtue.

> Then he is instructed in what is above him. He learns
> that his being is without bound; that to the good, to the
> perfect, he is born, low as he now lies in evil and weakness.
> That which he venerates is still his own, though he has
> not realized it yet. (DSA)

The moral sentiment is aligned with virtue—"adherence in action to the nature of things"—and links us to the positive, renewing power of the creation. This synchrony leads to increased feelings of stability and belonging in the universe. "The dawn of the sentiment of virtue in the heart is the assurance that Law is . . . sovereign over all natures," Waldo wrote. Then "the worlds, time, space, eternity, do seem to break out in joy." It is through this beatitude that "the soul first knows itself," revealed by the joy at the heart of creation (DSA).

Waldo described the soul as a discarnate body that accompanies a person through life, much like genius guides you toward self-realization. Soul is the essence that never abandons you and reminds you of your divine origin. For Stoics like Marcus Aurelius, the soul was a "sphere in equilibrium," a unity balanced and made whole through self-remembrance; the fruit of neither grasping at things nor retreating inward; the result of not losing oneself in the external world, but—in the desire for self-knowledge—becoming "ablaze with light and looking at the truth, without and within."[14] Waldo knew that the soul "refuses limits and always affirms an optimism never a pessimism," and he believed moral sentiment to be the language of that optimism, which provides "insight of this perfection of the laws of the soul" (*C*).

His observation that soul manifests differently in different endeavors is especially astute. According to Waldo, when the soul "breathes through intellect it is genius. When it breathes through . . . will, it is virtue. And when it flows through . . . affection, it is love" (*O*). The soul moves us toward excellence, which is not always visible to the eye of the ego. ("Its operation in life, though slow to the senses, is well-known to the soul.") The "rapid intrinsic energy [that] worketh everywhere, righting wrongs, correcting appearances, and bringing facts to the harmony with thoughts," is evidence of soul (*DSA*).

To the degree that we ignore the soulful dimension, we fall into mediocrity, and well-being plummets. "The absence of this primary faith is the presence of degradation" (*DSA*). This is what we see today, a soul-deprived, spiritually degraded culture in which the quest for self-knowledge is rarely a priority. Waldo drew attention to the roots of this moral collapse, sprouting in America, being nourished by passivity and materialism. "The doctrine of the divine nature is forgotten," he wrote, "and sickness infects and dwarfs [our] constitution."

> Once man was all; now he is an appendage, a nuisance. . . .
> The doctrine of inspiration is lost. . . . Miracles, prophecy,
> poetry, the ideal life, the holy life, exist as ancient history
> merely; they are not in the belief, nor in the aspiration of
> society; but, when suggested, seem ridiculous. (*DSA*)

When this moral sentiment falls out of favor, the "high ends of being fade out of sight, and life becomes 'comic or pitiful.'" We grow ever more myopic and superficial, sensitive to "what addresses the senses," and oblivious of what transcends them. This is seminal to the pessimistic orientation. Marcus Aurelius compared such nearsightedness to a man who looks at a fresh spring but sees only a stagnant swamp. Rather than drink from its clear, sweet depths, he curses the spring even as it bubbles up from its source. He can shovel mud into it, or dung, and the stream will carry it away, wash itself clean, remain unstained. "Not a cistern but a perpetual spring," Marcus Aurelius wrote.[15] In other words, a pessimist can dump as much waste into his mind stream as he likes, but the sluicing of nature will clear it away and show him (if he's willing to look) the error of his thinking.

The spiritual practice of self-inquiry enables us to cut through the muck. Philosophical questions form a cognitive net that permits you to sift through the contents of your mind, isolate the problem parts, and examine what you find there. Upsetting as this sifting can be, it is the unavoidable price of wisdom. Waldo viewed self-inquiry as a form of spiritual hygiene and reminds us that every step taken on the path of self-knowledge is its own reward. His friend Henry likened this process to a dog chomping down on a bone. The meat it's digging for is self-knowledge. "Know what you love," Thoreau wrote. "Know your own bone; gnaw it, bury it, unearth it, and bury it still."[16] This turning inward away from the external whirlwind allows insight to dawn. You see with utmost clarity that you are responsible for your own happiness and—though you may be victimized by circumstances—you remain a victim by choice. This responsibility can feel overwhelming; on braver days, it's a great relief. The impulse to explore inner and outer reality, to discover how things work, saves us from sorrow and stagnation.

Science and Optimism

Before the publication, in 1859, of *On the Origin of Species*, Waldo was applying certain of Darwin's evolutionary principles to the sphere of self-development. The aspirational spirit of science mirrors Waldo's understanding of the mind as metamorphic, dynamic, and driven by forces beyond our reckoning. Waldo saw no conflict between acknowledging science's grasp of material reality and remembering the awareness of an unknown metaphysical source.

For him, science was a subset of spirituality. Like spiritual seekers, scientists are driven by experimentation and the desire to illuminate the truth. Seekers and scientists long to peel back the layers that conceal reality and peer into its depths. Physical evolution points to an analogous process in the spiritual sphere, Waldo believed. While we've made great leaps in physical organization and knowledge over eons of geological time, we've yet to approach that level of mastery and dedication to spiritual development, and that could be the death of us.

Science is a front seat to mystery—as is spiritual practice—one that

corrects old creeds [and] sweeps away, with every new perception, our infantile catechisms, and necessitates a faith commensurate with the grander orbits and universal laws which it discloses. Yet it does not surprise the moral sentiment. That was older and awaited expectant these larger insights. (*TAS*)

To help us maintain our balance within the cosmos, science must remember that it is in service to nature, not vice versa. The scientist risks mistaking herself for God otherwise, a slippery ethical slope that has already yielded some awful results. When science is viewed as the true religion, we forget who, or what, is in control. We conveniently overlook the fact that "nature who made the mason, made the house" (*N*). For science to fulfill its spiritual function, the false divide between nature and spirit must be quashed once and for all; also, the parochial belief that science constitutes the zenith of human endeavor, making scientific mastery as close to godliness as we can get. It subtracts nothing from our esteem for the brilliance of science to remember that science has its limits. As a spiritual teacher once said to me, "The mind cannot know what's beyond the mind." Waldo explained that "every natural fact" is the symbol of some spiritual fact; "Every appearance in nature corresponds to some state of mind" (*N*).

Where others focused on divisive details, Waldo leapfrogged academic categories and saw unifying patterns everywhere. Long before he knew about natural selection, for example, he'd been impressed by the sacrifices nature makes in her abundant reproductive output.

The vegetable life does not content itself with casting from the flower or tree a single seed, but it fills the air with a

> prodigality of seeds, that, if thousands perish, thousands
> may plant themselves, that hundreds may come up, that
> tens may live to maturity; that, at least one may replace the
> parent. (*N*)

This profligacy was a proof for hope, he believed. It's the core of the optimist's worldview. Nature is fecund and endlessly inventive, mirroring *in us* the ingenuity of her creative process. Artists and creators of all kinds spawn multitudes of ideas, the bulk of which do not survive, on the path to bringing new life into the world, and experiment with diverse methods in the process of making something. Those who wish to marry for love, and create a family, typically cast wide romantic nets on the path to finding a compatible mate. Spiritual seekers knock on many doors and test numerous teachings before choosing one whose practice suits them and quickens their unfolding.

When Waldo wrote about this dynamic, he might have been describing the Hindu gods Shiva and Shakti giving birth to the multiverse.

> That famous aboriginal push propagates itself through all
> the balls of the system; through every atom of every ball;
> through all the races of creatures, and through the history
> and performance of every individual. (*N*)

He's giving voice to the primal thrust of creation, nature burning with the energy of life. He might have been anticipating the discoveries by Einstein, Schrödinger, and others concerning matter and energy, and how the two are one. "Compound it how she will, star, sand, fire, water, tree, man, it is still one stuff, and betrays the same properties," he wrote. "Without electricity, the air would rot" (*N*). Our aspiration as seekers rots equally fast when we fail to recharge our batteries.

Choosing hope over defeat is medicinal. The reason that science has such a soul-saving effect is that it speaks to the explorer in us, the adventurer, the hero. Science reminds us of the unseen world beyond our physical senses. When we keep the door of our minds ajar, opened out on the infinite, hope can breathe. Why else would nations with pressing humanitarian needs spend billions of dollars on space exploration? Who needs helicopters on Mars when children are starving and the planet is under threat? The answer is spiritual not rational. Space travel satisfies our collective need to transcend our limits, move toward the unknown, break free. We're a claustrophobic species that depends on risk and imagination for its spiritual survival. We would freeze in existential shock otherwise or suffocate under an avalanche of accumulated anxiety and pessimism. The ability to extend ourselves, to experience awe, saves us from entrapment. Scientists and seekers are dedicated to the proposition of keeping this human escape hatch open. "Men love to wonder, and that is the seed of our science," Waldo wrote (*WAD*). Awe is the bridge between man and God.

✎ THE BRIEF ✎

Realistic optimism is central to self-reliance. This form of optimism does not pretend that all will be well, and we'll live happily ever after. Nor does realistic optimism deny the facts on the ground, including the need to be vigilant about human destructiveness and evil. Optimism rests on a humble awareness of our limited knowledge and ability to predict the future; also, the fact that everything in nature is constantly changing. Misfortune can lead to hopeful results, and destruction may lead to new forms of growth. Pessimism can lead to arrogance and is often a failure of the imagination. Though fixated hope based on specific outcomes isn't helpful, spiritual hope is lifesaving and helps you stay open to unexpected turns of fortune and new potential. The "moral sentiment" enables you to maintain connection with your better angels and the soul that refuses limits. Virtue elevates the sinking mind and reminds it of its divine origins, which are ever-expanding. As an outgrowth of the aspirational spirit, science is optimistic by nature, a path for seeking truth, dispelling illusion, and nourishing our need for exploration as well as freedom from the tyranny of ignorance. Only when the spiritual underpinnings of science are forgotten—and the scientist confuses herself with God—does science pose a threat to our well-being.

On Awe

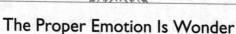

The Proper Emotion Is Wonder

"The earth laughs in flowers."

Express Your Astonishment

In the spring of 1871, Waldo traveled to the western United States with the goal of visiting Yosemite National Park. His motivation was twofold: to behold the marvel of El Capitan, the great summit at the center of the park, and to meet a thirty-three-year-old ex–mill hand named John Muir whose reputation had reached him in Concord.

Muir had become the patron saint of Yosemite since his arrival there three years earlier. The native Scotsman had been traveling west to San Francisco when he stopped in the valley, fell rapturously in love with the landscape, and decided to make it his home.

"This valley is the only place that comes up to its brag about it," he wrote in his journal. Muir described "[scrambling] down steep cliff faces to get a closer look at the waterfalls, whooping and howling at the vistas, jumping tirelessly from flower to flower."[1] He constructed a small cabin along Yosemite Creek and spent his days in the backcountry, surrounded by majestic beauty, accompanied only by "a tin cup, a handful of tea, a loaf of bread, and a copy of Emerson."[2]

When Muir learned of his literary hero's imminent arrival, he was too starstruck to approach Waldo in person. As he remembered later,

> I was excited as I had never been excited before, and my heart throbbed as if an angel direct from heaven had alighted on the Sierran rocks. But so great was my awe and reverence, I did not dare to go to him or speak to him.[3]

Instead, Muir left Waldo a note with an offer to serve as his local guide. Waldo was delighted. For the next five days, the two wandered around the valley together, Muir holding forth on Yosemite's natural wonders and seventy-one-year-old Waldo doing his best to keep up. The strapping Scotsman was as knowledgeable about nature as Henry had been, and Waldo was delighted to find at the end of his career the prophet-naturalist he had called for so long ago.

For Muir, Waldo's visit was a "laying on of hands," a benediction of his work from a literary giant. The following spring, Muir wrote to his new friend in an effort to lure him back to the valley.

"You cannot be content with last year's baptism," he promised Waldo.

> T'was only a sprinkle. Come be immersed. . . . Think of the soul lavings and bathings you will get. . . . Think of the glow of your afterlife . . . Here are the shores of all our eternities. . . . Here we may more easily see God.[4]

Muir and Emerson were joined by their wonder and a shared mission to "save the American soul from total surrender to materialism," as the new immigrant put it.[5] Muir feared that the country's natural riches would cause the nation to "grow too fast for its virtue and its peace" and that "the western lands instead of being held as a national treasure to be used prudently and lawfully would be pillaged by an accursed tribe of barbarous robbers."[6] They shared the conviction that greed threatened to subvert God's plan for America, that their country's spirit would only be preserved by way of a widespread awakening of reverence and awe.

Though Muir's chosen locale was stupendous and rare, Waldo made it clear that majestic surroundings are unnecessary for a person to be astonished by the splendor of this mysterious world. "The invariable mark of wisdom is to see the miraculous in the common," he taught (N). Such wonder is only possible when we pay undivided attention to our experience and take the time to reflect on its impact. "When the act of reflection takes place in the mind, when we look at ourselves in the light of thought," we rediscover the magic of the world, Waldo wrote (SL). When we stop to pay witness to our experience without distraction, it is more

than enough to leave us astonished; a single moment of lucid seeing can cleave the heart, and open the mind, of even the most
hardened cynic. The staunchest materialist ("a sturdy capitalist")
would turn transcendentalist in a heartbeat, Waldo suggested, if
he turned from the ledger sheet of his life to the mystery spread
out in every direction before him. The scales would be lifted from
his eyes after perceiving that "no matter how deep and square on
blocks of Quincy granite" his house's foundation was laid, the ordinary world he imagined was an illusion. He would grasp that
the edifice of his existence was set at last

> not on a cube corresponding to the angles of his structure
> [but on] . . . a mass of unknown materials and solidity,
> red-hot or white-hot perhaps at the core, which rounds off
> to an almost perfect sphericity, and lies floating in soft air,
> and goes spinning away, dragging bank and banker with
> it at a rate of thousands of miles an hour, he knows not
> whither . . . (*T*)

Going about our daily lives, believing we know where we stand,
we are actually dancing on the surface of a "bit of bullet now
glimmering, now darkling through a small cubic space on the
edge of an unimaginable pit of emptiness" (*T*). Awe belies our vision of a flattened, domesticated world where we are brainwashed
to think small in the de-geniusing process of growing up. Wonder
is always available to us when we ride this "wild balloon" with
open eyes. Few can fail to be overcome by the unlikely miracle of
our existence when we're paying attention. "How we came out of

silence into this sounding world is the wonder of wonder," Waldo wrote. "All other marvels are less." Only when we meet our brief lives with wonder do they become truly meaningful. We should "express our astonishment before we are swallowed up in the yeast of the abyss, to lift up our hands and say Kosmos."[7]

The ancient Greeks used the word *kosmos* to denote a particular kind of splendor, equal parts order and beauty. For them as for Waldo, beauty is a glimpse of eternity through a material lens, a portal to higher consciousness. "Into every beautiful object, there enters somewhat immeasurable and divine," Waldo tells us. When this happens, "a *second sight* is opened," revealing that all things have their singular loveliness. "There is no object so foul that intense light will not make it beautiful" (*B*).

> This homely game of life we play, covers, under what seem foolish details, principles that astonish. (*DSA*)

Our minds brighten or dim in accordance to our willingness to be astonished. This prepares the way for "lustres," as Waldo called them, those flashes of heightened awareness that elevate the mind. The great turning points in our lives are not events, he tells us, but moments of illumination that change how we see.

Time Stops

Illuminating moments transform us by arresting the discursive mind and changing our habitual sense of time. The shock of being where we are—fully—awakens our senses and alerts perception to the vastness of the "eternal present." So different is this wakefulness from our ordinary way of seeing that "casting moments" such as these become indelible, reminding us of something we seem to have forgotten. Waldo explained that when the mind goes still, we touch into the "deep power in which we live, whose beatitude is all accessible to us" (*O*). Illusory obstacles fall from view in this brightened state, revealing the nondual nature of being. Then "the act of seeing and things seen, the seer and the spectacle, the subject and the object are one" (*O*). Waldo taught that these experiences are natural and increase in frequency as the seeker tunes in to their frequency. "I hold that ecstasy will be found normal," Waldo prophesied, "an example of a higher plane of the same gentle gravitation by which stones fall and rivers run" (*INS*).

In the 1950s, American psychologist Abraham Maslow studied elevated states of consciousness in his groundbreaking work with peak experiences. Inspired by the insights of William James, Maslow helped legitimize awe and wonder as serious subjects for scientific research. Though he'd have rejected the mantle of *transcendentalist*, and he resisted defining peak experiences as spiritual in nature, Maslow's observations bear striking similarities to Waldo's philosophy. Maslow studied thousands of patients over a thirty-year period and found that peak experiences generate what he called "an advanced form of perceiving reality . . . mystic and magical in their effect upon the experiencer."[8] What's more, these transcendent peak experiences bring grounded, life-enhancing benefits. A peak experiencer is likely to perceive himself as the responsible, active, "creative center" of his activities more than at other times, according to Maslow:

like a prime-mover, more self-determined (rather
than caused, dependent, passive, weak). He feels himself
to be his own boss, fully responsible, fully volitional,
with more "free-will" than at other times, master of his
fate, an agent.[9]

Maslow used the term Being Cognition (B-Cognition) to describe the shift in cognition among experiencers, as opposed to
the Deprivation Cognition (D-Cognition) we experience in ordinary life. In B-Cognition, one experiences an altered relationship to time and space; also feelings of wholeness and harmony,
liberation from interior conflict, and the sense that one is using
all her capacities and capabilities to their highest potential. A person feels herself to be functioning effortlessly, without strain or
struggle. Maslow explained that during B-Cognition, a person is
more spontaneous and expressive, displaying "naturally flowing
behavior that is not constrained by conformity." Newly open to
creative ideas, keenly aware of the present "without influence of
the past or expected future experiences," a person experiencing
B-Cognition becomes flexible, free, and attentive in startling, un-
forgettable ways.[10]

There are many doorways to this timeless dimension: meditation, yoga, prayer, chanting, ecstatic movement, psychedelics,
extreme suffering, physical exertion, sexual intimacy, aesthetic
experience. Whatever method you use to help pause the thinking
mind, they serve a similar purpose: to open yourself to the eternal
present. I had a profound experience of timelessness at a saint's
grave site in India thirty years ago. I was standing in line with a
hundred other pilgrims to visit the grave of this long-dead master

in Pondicherry. Ahead of me in the line was a German mother helping her disabled child kneel at the side of the marble tomb. The boy, no more than twelve or so, was having a hard time bending his knees. Finally, she helped him to the ground and rested his forehead against the tomb. I watched the expression on the boy's face soften, felt the cold marble under my feet, smelled the flowers blanketing the tomb; then a great silence seemed to settle over my mind, pulling me into a profound state of relaxation. I felt the moment pulsing inside me, alive, intense, and completely *full*. No mind babble existed between me and the world; I was there but also beyond there, watching this scene as if through an enlarged aperture.

Eventually, the boy opened his eyes and stood up with his mother's help. My eyes fell on a bunch of marigolds strewn near the saint's picture at the head of the tomb. They seemed to shine with a light that caused them to stand out from everything else, drawing me into their shimmering orangeness. I had the strong experience of time stopping. I came across a passage, years later, written by a man who'd been part of the first team to scale Mount Everest, which recalled this moment in India. When the mountaineer was returning from the peak, he paused to take in the stupendous view, turned his eyes to the ground, and saw a small blue flower in the snow.

I don't know how to describe what happened. Everything opened up and flowed together and made some strange kind of sense, and I was at complete peace. I have no idea how long I stood there. It could have been minutes or hours. Time melted. But when I came down, my life was different.[11]

Our susceptibility to wonder matters more than our location, Waldo knew. The most humdrum encounters can deliver us "lustres." After visiting an elderly Quaker lady named Mary Rotch one afternoon in 1836, Waldo had such an unexpected awakening. Alone in the parlor following their encounter, "I opened my eyes and let what would pass through them into the soul," he wrote in his journal.

> I saw no more my relation to Cambridge or Boston.
> I heeded no more what minute or hour the . . . clocks
> indicated. I saw only the noble earth on which I was born
> with the great star that warms and enlightens it. The pines
> glittered and challenged me to read their riddle, the oak
> leaves turned their somersaults, the wind bustled high
> overhead.[12]

Beyond the tick-tock of the timekeeping, worried mind, this transcendent perspective is always available. But it is so pervasive and integral that it escapes our attention most of the time. This is where awe comes in. When we wonder, the mind goes quiet, whether we're immersed in nature, listening to music, enjoying art, playing with children, making love, bonding with others in joy or sorrow, or gazing up at the naked sky; an inner window slides open providing entrée to a luminous world beyond our ordinary vision. We cannot engineer awe, but awe-inspiring moments can be *invited* when we create conditions that quiet the mind and pay attention to this higher awareness.

The field of positive psychology, which grew directly out of Maslow's research, has a lot to say about awe. Experiences of awe have been linked to prosocial behavior, critical thinking, heightened physiological functioning (including lowered stress, increased immune function, and decreased rates of arthritis, diabetes, clinical depression, and heart disease).[13] Awe is nature's alarm clock, shaking us out of our workaday trance and revealing the magnificence of the world *as it is.* We're sensitized, grounded, made whole. Waldo lived a good deal of his life in this state.

> I see the spectacle of morning from the hilltop over my house, from daybreak till sunrise, with emotions that an angel might share. (*N*)

This sacramental view transforms how we live, infusing ordinary moments with an awareness of God.

We're all mystics in the making, after all; awe is a part of our biological human repertoire. Experiences of timelessness, non-linearity, and sacredness are as universal as laughter and eating. As French philosopher Louis Claude de Saint-Martin reminds us, "All mystics speak the same language, for they come from the same country."[14] This is our common origin, the One Mind where we are connected, our spiritual home. We learn to recognize this awe-inspired quality in others and seek out their company. This proves that wonder, like all emotions, is contagious. As emotional intelligence pioneer Daniel Goleman told me, "We catch each other's emotions like a cold." This contagion applies to awe as well.

Goleman first noticed this contagious quality while study-ing spiritual practitioners in India as a post-doctoral student at Harvard. Acknowledged masters were "lively and engaged, extremely present, involved in the moment, often funny, yet profoundly at peace—equanimous in disturbing situations," Goleman noticed. They defied the stereotype of mystics as de-tached and otherworldly; in fact, the quality they exuded—known as *sukha* in Sanskrit—brought unusual presence. "You always felt better than before you'd spent time with them, and this feeling lasted," Goleman told me.

Maslow embodied some of these qualities himself, according to people who knew him. He was a man overflowing with pas-sion, curiosity, compassion, generosity, and love. The longer he ex-posed himself to peak experiencers, the happier Maslow seemed to have become. A moody kid from Brooklyn, burdened with a colossal mother complex, he became an ambassador of wonder and awe through his work on human potential. "The fact is that self-actualizing people are simultaneously the most individual-istic and the most altruistic and social and loving of all human beings," Maslow came to believe.[15] A comparable self-healing pro-cess had occurred in Waldo's life, evolving from a melancholic, self-hating ne'er-do-well into a remarkable spiritual human being. Even Nathaniel Hawthorne, his Anti-Transcendentalist neigh-bor, was struck by the quality of contagious wonder emanating from Waldo as a middle-aged man, a "gleam diffusing about his presence like a garment of a shining one."[16] Spanish philosopher George Santayana made a similar observation:

People flocked to him and listened to his word not for the sake of its absolute meaning as for the atmosphere of candor, purity, and serenity that hung about it, as about a sort of sacred music. They felt themselves in the presence of a rare and beautiful spirit who was in communion with a higher world.[17]

Shock and Awe

While today's generation ought to be the most awestruck in history—having mapped the human genome, traveled to outer space, connected electronically to the rest of the planet—we appear to be moving away from wonder. We're numbed by extraordinary technological feats, overcome by choice, and unable to regain our sense of awe. As addicts of newness, variety, and instant gratification, we're suffering from a growing anhedonia, struggling to feel deep satisfaction in the midst of all this innovation. As Jewish theologian Abraham Joshua Heschel put it, "We are shocked by the weakness of our awe, but also by the weakness of our shock."[18] Consumerism offers us lots of pleasure but not much joy, a wealth of information but not much wisdom, a great deal of novelty but not much awe.

When awe is diminished, anxiety proliferates. Fear narrows the mind, as we've learned, blocking the pathways to well-being. Wonder opens your sensory portals and allows the transcendent to enter in. Deprivation Cognition shrinks reality down to data points, obscuring the magnificent whole. Being Cognition returns spirituality to its proper place at the center of our existence, reversing our secular tendency to define reality in materialist terms. "We have a mental habit which makes it easier for us to explain the miraculous in natural terms than to explain the natural in the miraculous," as T. S. Eliot wrote. "This is the cause of our spiritual downfall."[19]

As a mystic, Waldo knew that a dimension exists wherein double-blind experiments are irrelevant, where reality outstrips our weights and measures, and this knowledge has the power to prompt radical change in how a person lives her life. "If your eye is on the eternal, your opinions and actions will have a beauty which no learning or combined advantages or other men can rival," he tells us (B). In this awe-opened space, new meanings, perceptions, capacities, dreams, possibilities, powers, and insights are born in you. You're able to draw new mental maps of the world and imagine novel ways forward. Novelist James Joyce defined epiphany as "the sudden recognition of the significance of trivial things."[20] You feel the harmony inherent to nature, which attunes you to the rhythms of the spirit as well.

Mysticism articulates this harmony. It is the expression of "the tendency of the human spirit towards complete harmony with the transcendental order," in the words of scholar Evelyn Underhill.[21] When the values of a society contradict or obstruct this harmony, destruction is sure to follow. The higher tier of our emotions—awe, wonder, revelation, epiphany—are made to appear exotic in our culture, like specialty items on the menu of human experience rather than the main course. Writer Frederick Buechner described this imbalance well as regards his own worldly life. "We are all of us more mystics than we believe or choose to believe," Buechner wrote.

> Life is complicated enough as it is, after all. Through some moment of beauty or pain, some sudden turning in our lives, we catch glimmers at least of what the saints are blinded by; only then, unlike the saints, we tend to go on as though nothing has happened.[22]

To go on as if something *has* happened, Buechner continued, is to enter the dimension of life "that religion is a word for." Waldo's overarching message to us is *live your life as if something has happened*. Don't miss out on the magical parts. Maslow believed that the tale of the human race "is the story of men and women selling themselves short," and this is how we shortchange our potential.[23] We're more frightened by the prospect of transcendence and freedom than we are of failure. Though we're afraid to know "the fearsome and unsavory parts of ourselves . . . we fear even more to know the godlike in ourselves," Maslow wrote.[24] We overcome this fear by remembering that we're spiritual beings first, capitalists, consumers, and materialists second.

The soul is roused from its slumber by awe, and when this happens it starts to shine. Dropping the veil of ignorance, we see that we are nothing *but* God and that the highest act of which we are capable is adoration. Attuned to harmony and wonder, we see the world through the eyes of God. In a famous passage, Waldo described having such a cosmic vision while walking one day on

Boston Common, when reality revealed its dazzling face and linked him to the Over-Soul.

> Standing on the bare ground,—my head bathed by the blithe air and uplifted into infinite space,—all mean egotism vanishes. I become a transparent eyeball; I am nothing; I see all; the currents of the Universal Being circulate through me; I am part and parcel of God. (*N*)

The same is true for each one of us.

～ THE BRIEF ～

Awe is the alarm clock installed by nature to awaken you to the wonder of being. Without awe, your life is diminished; you forget the sacred dimension of existence and the miraculous nature of this earthly experience. The upper reaches of human emotions—wonder, awe, elevation, astonishment, rapture, adoration, and transcendence—are critical to flourishing; without these higher emotions, we forget who we are, as spiritual beings, and risk sinking into despair. Perception is diminished when you view existence through a material lens and focus on the exterior life. In awe-filled moments, time seems to stop, dropping you into the eternal present, heightening awareness, increasing sensitivity, making these interludes indelible in memory. In this awe-opened space, new ideas, visions, and inspirations take place, creating the conditions of transformation. Peak experiences happen in unexpected moments and cannot be engineered, though their likelihood can be increased through concerted attention to the present moment. The miracles of technology (and modern life, generally) sometimes conspire against wonder and awe by shrinking attention, promoting distraction, and spoiling the simplicity of life with too much variety, too many choices, and too many ways to avoid being present.

LESSON TWELVE

On Enlightenment

Your Giant Goes with You
Wherever You Go

"Know yourself a man and be a god."

Rational Transcendence

Waldo began "Self-Reliance" with the Latin maxim, *Ne te quae-siveris extra*: Do not seek outside yourself. He was reminding us without equivocation that what we're searching for through religion is already inside us. This blasphemy turned Waldo into public enemy number one within the church he had rejected. Insult was added to injury after his scandalous Harvard Divinity School address, which caused him to be excommunicated from his alma mater for the next thirty years.

Waldo had been invited to speak to a handful of undergraduates preparing for the ministry, but rather than encouraging them in their liturgical studies, he warned the boys that religious education was unnecessary and that what they were being taught by the clergy was nonsense. Contradicting church doctrine, he assured them that communicating with God was an inside job (no intermediary necessary), that dogma sabotages devotion, and that direct spiritual experience is far more valuable than anything they would find in scripture. Waldo urged his teenaged audience to cast off their clerical ambitions and study the gospel of nature instead.

Rather than wait for God's light to be revealed to them by religious authorities, they should first acknowledge the light already in them, waiting to be discovered. "Let me admonish you, first of all, to go alone," he told them. "Refuse the good models, even those most sacred in the imagination of men, and dare to love God without mediator or veil" (*DSA*). We can only imagine how confusing this message must have been to the seminary boys! Waldo was happy to deliver this blow, and his rebel fury never left him, serving him exceedingly well on the lecture circuit, where he could speak his mind without restraint to audiences eager to think for themselves and pursue the transcendentalist path. To his adult listeners, he made it perfectly clear that self-reliance is a spiritual practice of empowerment through connection with the divine. Self-reliance is reliance on God, he told them. Although we may be "gods in ruins," our crumbling edifices are forever sacred at their foundation. Though we betray our own potential daily, our baseline divinity is undiminished. Each individual is "the façade of a temple wherein all wisdom and good abide," and though many of Waldo's fans were undoubtedly dubious, he never stopped reminding them of their own hidden identity (*O*).

God speaks to humankind *through* nature—*as* nature—as we've learned, pacifying the turbulent mind. We learn to calibrate our rhythms to those of the natural world and experience the sacredness of life in the body. "Spirit builds itself a house, and beyond its house a world, and beyond its world a heaven," he explained (*N*). This heavenly abode of enlightened awareness is erected through conscious, and meticulous, ongoing efforts to discover the truth of who we are. This self-awakening process was described by the original Stoics as "rational transcendence," which, in order to increase in strength, requires that we overcome our self-centeredness.

The ancients (and Waldo too) defined reason differently than we do today. In their understanding, reason relates not only to analytical thought but also to the capacity to observe our lives from the witness perspective. This awareness makes it possible to reflect upon experience, optimize conditions with self-knowledge, find meaning in our existence, and strengthen spiritual awareness through targeted practice.

The Stoics believed that it is reason that gives form and meaning to the cosmos and makes enlightenment possible, and that "rational transcendence" is achieved by linking one's individual mind to the One Mind of God. They emphasized that this alignment requires a commitment that is rare among people who eschew self-encounter. This turning away from self-knowledge is humanity's tragic flaw, causing untold suffering and ignorance to multiply down through the ages. Waldo viewed this tragedy in exactly the same way. Fifty years after his death, British writer Aldous Huxley (a distant cousin of Waldo's) addressed this conundrum directly.

> It is because we don't know who we are, because we are unaware that the Kingdom of Heaven is within us, that we behave in the generally silly, the often insane, the sometimes criminal ways that are so characteristically human.[1]

Huxley was a cosmic optimist himself, whose hope was grounded in the possibility of rational transcendence. "We are saved by, we are liberated and enlightened, by perceiving the hitherto unperceived good that is already within us," wrote Huxley, "by returning to our eternal ground and returning where, without knowing it, we have always been."[2]

Reason is necessary for this spiritual rebalancing to take place. Waldo explained,

> He who knows that power is inborn, that he is weak because he has looked for good out of him [and] throws himself unhesitatingly on his [reason], instantly rights himself, stands in the erect position, commands his limbs, works miracles; just as a man who stands on his feet is stronger than a man who stands on his head. (*SR*)

By strengthening our minds and hearts, we're able to stop living upside down. We learn to assume the "erect position" and bring out what is best inside us. This aspiration is linked to the Greek ideal of *arete*, which translates as "excellence." As psychologist Jonathan Haidt points out, the *arete* of a knife is to cut well. The *arete* of an eye is to see well. And the *arete* of a human being is to live an awakened, self-reliant life.[3]

Excellence includes an awareness of the transcendental dimension. Without this soul perspective, it's impossible to appreciate the enormity of this astounding creation and our part within it. *Arete* speaks to the giant within us, that "immensity [which is] not possessed and that cannot be possessed," in Waldo's words (*O*). This giant is comparable to a trillion-watt light bulb blazing at your core. "From within or from behind, the light shines through us upon things, and makes us aware that we are nothing, but the light is all," he tells us.

> Language cannot paint it with his colors. It is too subtle. It is undefinable, unmeasurable, but we know that it pervades and contains us. We know that all spiritual being is in man. (*O*)

There's a striking parallel between this passage and Einstein's reported description of human beings as "slowed down sound and light waves, a walking bundle of frequencies tuned into the cosmos." "We are souls dressed up in sacred biochemical garments and our bodies are the instruments through which our souls play our music," Einstein wrote.[4] This light illuminates what Waldo called "the infinitude of the private man," revealing that personality (the exterior life) is always the foreground, never the background. This knowledge is paradoxically empowering; the personal ego takes on its true proportion against the immensity, illuminated by the "principle which is the basis of all things," the "simple, quiet, undescribed, indescribable presence, dwelling very peacefully inside us" (*W*).

When you tap into this unified field, you become comically aware of your diminutive stature in the great web of being. You're also reminded of the necessity for spiritual surrender. "[You] are not to do, but to let do. Not to work but be worked upon," he tells us (*W*). When we allow conditions to unfold as they will, we gain "vast and sudden powers," the greatest of which is motherwit—practical, commonsense intelligence—which is the cure for "false theology" in Waldo's estimation. "Forget your books and traditions and obey your moral perceptions [of the] hour" (*W*).

Action that is elevated by motherwit ennobles our endeavors, while ambition without humility devolves into willful, selfish striving. A devotion to the exterior life dooms us to mediocrity and conformity. "It's a capital mistake to seek greatness by following the great," he reminds us, or base our success on gaining advantage over another. Self-reliance reminds us that "the fountain of all good [is] within" ourselves, and that you "equally with every man [are] an inlet into the deeps of Reason" (*DSA*). Rational transcendence heals the wound of separation that seems to exist between ourselves and God.

Stop Worshipping the Past

It is imperative not to subordinate ourselves or our accomplishments to what has been achieved before. Rumination, nostalgia, and fealty to the past are against nature, since every moment is fresh and new. The past is "swallowed and forgotten," while the "coming only is sacred" (*CIR*).

Rather than imitate the dead, we must focus on becoming *ourselves*. "Nothing is secure but life, transition, the energizing spirit," Waldo taught. Retrospection can lead to self-sabotage, stagnation, and "universal decay . . . [the] death of faith in society" (*CIR*). Overreliance on tradition blocks progress and gives rise to fundamentalist theology and fascism, as we are witnessing today. At this writing, the Taliban takeover in Afghanistan has forced its citizens (especially women and girls) to live by fourteenth-century religious laws or suffer barbaric consequences. White supremacists are militarizing around the United States in favor of an idealized America where segregation between races is reinstated, marriage must be heterosexual, gun sales are unlimited, and the Constitution—a document created three centuries ago by (mostly) slaveholding white men—is consecrated as the word of God.

Attempts to reinstate bigotries from eras past are as dangerous as they are futile. Religiosity is pitted against spirituality, and holy scriptures are used to perpetuate moral crimes. To keep ourselves alive spiritually, each of us must follow the dictates of her faith into her own kind of worship, to leave off looking to the past for signs of the future. Discovering your own relationship to spirit is far more demanding than following in the footsteps of tradition. A personal spirituality forces you to stand on your own clay feet on the path to uncovering the light within. Such spiritual self-reliance is the basis of Stoic philosophy. Waldo understood the challenges of this personal approach. "Was never stoicism so stern and exigent as this shall be," he wrote.

> It shall send man home to his central solitude, shame these
> social, supplicating manners, and make him know that
> much of the time he must have himself to his friend. (*W*)

In other words, we must trust ourselves to stand alone in the
presence of God. This is a frightening proposition for many
churchgoers ("Not knowing what else to do, we ape our ancestors" [*W*]). Waldo has harsh words for people who choose to
abdicate their spiritual authority. Organized religions "stagger
backward to mummeries of the dark ages" and cater to congre-
gations who have

> faith in chemistry, in meat, in wine, in wealth, in
> machinery, in the steam-engine, galvanic battery, turbine-
> wheels, sewing machines, and in public opinion, but not
> in divine causes. (*W*)

Christianity had failed miserably in its transformative mission,
he maintained. It was out of gas, spiritually speaking, a situation
that persists today. A recent Pew Research poll on the number
of Americans who affiliate with no religion was higher than at
any time in the poll's history, although nearly three-quarters of
participants claimed to believe in God, and another forty percent
described themselves as "spiritual but not religious."[5] "[In] a transition period [when] the old faiths which comforted nations . . .
seem to have spent their force," and where we see lost souls cir-
cling everywhere, Waldo observed as if speaking to our current
spiritual crisis, "a whole population of gentlemen and ladies

[are] out in search of religion," yet coming up frequently empty-handed. "[The] population is godless, materialized,—no bond, no fellow-feeling, no enthusiasm" (*W*). This widespread anomie confounded Waldo ("How is it people manage to live on,—so aimless are they?"), though its cause was perfectly obvious. The "know-nothing religions [that] proscribe intellect" were to blame, without a doubt: those "slave-holding and slave-trading religions wherein the whiteness of the ritual covers scarlet indulgence" (*W*). Charlatans and plaster saints rush in to fill the void left behind by standard religions and only make things worse. Waldo might have been visiting some New Age expo when he described the spiritual circuses exploiting citizens' sincere longing for God, with their

> freak and extravagance, [the] peacock ritualism, the
> retrogression to Popery, the maundering of Mormons,
> the squalor of Mesmerism, the deliration of rappings, the
> rat and mouse revelation, thumps in table-drawers, and
> black arts. (*W*)

Hucksters thrive on the yearnings of seekers, as we know, and Waldo warned against sacrificing our discernment on the way to discovering an authentic path.

There are undeniable benefits to apostasy. Leaving the religion of your birth can ripen you tremendously for spiritual growth. As the scion of a family of ministers dating back to the *Mayflower*, Waldo's choice to leave the church was especially dramatic. When his explorations began outside the confines of the church, most of his family and friends were appalled. Aunt Mary compared Waldo's attraction to Eastern philosophy to joining a satanic cult. She condemned the "withering Lucifer doctrine of pantheism" infecting his mind, and feared that her nephew, "lost in the halo of his imagination," might never return to the fold (she was right).[6] Had Waldo not fallen in love with the Bhagavad Gita and immersed himself in nondual teachings, however, he would never have written "Self-Reliance." As for his devotion to Jesus, it remained unshakable throughout his lifetime. Waldo was contemptuous of the idolatrous dogma threatening to obscure Christ's message of universal love. It is important not to mistake religious authorities for the prophets whose vision they espouse in their churches.

> If a man claims to know and speak to God, and carries you
> backward to phraseology of some old mouldered nation
> in another country, in another world, believe him not.
> Is the acorn better than the oak which is its fulness and
> completion? Is the parent better than the child into whom
> he has cast his ripened being? Whence, then, this worship
> of the past? (SR)

When a church relegates revelation to antiquity, as something "long ago given and done as if God were dead," that institution is doomed to obsolescence (DSA). Religion's sole purpose is to facilitate our rapprochement with God within and provide tools for spiritual self-remembrance (which Plato called *anamnesis*). The rest of religious dogma is window dressing, theological folderol, that eclipses "the true Christianity." When this happens, "a faith like Christ's in the infinitude of man—is lost." In such a godless climate,

> none believeth in the soul of man, but only in some
> man or person old and departed. All men go in flocks
> to this saint or that poet, avoiding the God who seeth
> in secret.

Religious conformity gives rise to followers who "think society wiser than their soul, and know not that one soul, and their soul, is wiser than the whole world" (*DSA*).

We need a new creation story, Waldo explained, one that includes what we know about science and the physical universe. So long as faith traditions fashion themselves as bulwarks *against* progress and refuse to evolve with the times, spiritual degradation is sure to get worse. It is impossible to build a living faith on a moldy foundation of denial. "The irresistible effect of Copernican astronomy has been to make the great scheme of the salvation of man absolutely incredible," Waldo realized.[7] The current mass exodus from organized religion proves that antediluvian fairy tales no longer satisfy the contemporary seeker's desire for truth. ("The scientific mind must have a faith which is science" [*W*].) Waldo was convinced there is no contradiction between a scientific worldview and metaphysics. "The true meaning of spiritual is *real*" (my emphasis), he insisted, calling on the religious leaders of his time to update their sacred narratives.

> Let us have nothing now which is not its own evidence. . . .
> Let us not be pestered with assertions and half-truths, with
> emotions and snuffle. (*W*)

Only when contemporary knowledge is allowed can the transcendent reveal itself under the rubble of false beliefs. ("God builds his temple in the heart, on the ruins of churches and religions" [*W*].) This emerging, science-friendly faith asks that we put orthodoxy and obedience aside for the sake of spiritual honesty. Fortunately, the seeds of faith are already within us. "We are born believing," Waldo explained. "A man bears beliefs as a tree bears apples" (*W*). In the same way that hanging fruit only ripens in the present, nourished by the available sunlight, souls mature into their full sweetness only in the here and now, nourished by the light of deliberate attention. Waldo pointed to the example of flowers as demonstration of this point about the eternal now, the spiritual dimension beyond time, in one of his most famous passages.

> These roses under my window make no reference to
> former roses or to better ones. They are for what they
> are; they exist with God today. There is no time to them.
> There is simply the rose; it is perfect in every moment of
> its existence.

Now take two deep breaths before you continue.

> A man postpones or remembers; he does not exist in the
> present, but with reverted eye laments the past, or, heedless

of the riches that surround him, stands on tiptoe to foresee the future. He cannot be happy and strong until he too lives with nature in the present, above time. (*SR*)

It's fitting that in our harried, ADD culture, mindfulness practice has spread like wildfire.[8] We're starved for the eternal present, eager to touch into *nunc stans* (as opposed to the tick-tock of *nunc fluens*, or human-made temporality), as the ancients described the two kinds of time. But mindfulness practice is far from new in Western philosophy. Marcus Aurelius could have been channeling the mindfulness pioneer Dr. Jon Kabat-Zinn when he wrote,

> [The] person who applies all his attention and all his consciousness to the present will feel that he has everything within the present moment, for within this moment he has both the absolute value of existence and the absolute value of moral intent. There is nothing further left to desire. An entire lifetime and all eternity could not bring him more happiness.[9]

Waldo applied this simple, direct approach to his thoughts on faith. "They call it Christianity, I call it consciousness," he wrote.[10] The two great errors of historical Christianity—the mythologizing of Jesus and the fetishistic worship of the canonical Bible—interfere with direct connection to God, he maintained. Monotheistic faiths that only attribute divinity to God and his prophets (who happened to be male), while furiously denying it to the rest, are counterproductive and out of date. "That is always best which gives me to myself."

> The sublime is excited in me by the great stoical doctrine, *Obey thyself.* That which shows God in me, fortifies me. That which shows God out of me, makes me a wart and a wen. (*DSA*)

Spirit and biology are interconnected. Pierre Teilhard de Chardin, the French paleontologist-priest, suggested we should make this unity our primary object of contemplation if we hope to move toward the "Omega Point," in which all creation spirals toward a final point in unification.[11] This is comparable to the Stoic conception of the Logos, wherein "active reason" pervades and animates the universe, and all things are seen as parts of the whole.

Every molecule in nature houses the soul in miniature; the tiniest units of life contain God, and this spiritual consciousness pervades our very cells. When we consider our human condition through this unified, integrous lens, we see that virtue itself is natural and as intimate to us as our very breath. Waldo looked on "those sentiments which make the glory of the human being, love, humility, faith, as being also the intimacy of Divinity in the atoms" (*W*). This perspective builds confidence in our biological predisposition toward awakening to our true nature. It also helps us to gain

> assurances and previsions [that] emanate from the interior of his body and mind; as when flowers reach their ripeness, incense exhales from them. (*W*)

Imagine how extraordinary life would be if you lived with the awareness of this divine proximity. The spiritual giant within you would finally seem real. You could break out of the ego's straitjacket, push beyond your self-imposed limits, resist the pull of tribe and tradition, and know yourself to be wedded to all of creation.

Expanding the Circle

Saint Augustine, who read the Stoics as a young man in Algeria, described God as an infinite sphere "whose center is everywhere, its circumference nowhere."[12] Waldo believed much the same about human potential. "The life of man is a self-evolving circle, which, from a ring imperceptibly small, rushes on all sides outwards to new and larger circles, and that without end," he wrote (*CIR*).

How far we are able to expand depends on how self-reliant we become. "The extent to which this generation of circles, wheel without wheel, will go, depends on the forces or truth of the individual soul" (*CIR*). As we expand our circles, the ego is hollowed out, making room for the giant to stretch its limbs. Our personal narratives no longer define us. "The heart refuses to be imprisoned . . . in its first and narrowest pulses," Waldo explained, and "bends outward with a vast force, and to immense and innumerable expansion" (*CIR*).

The Stoic philosopher Hierocles believed that our task as individuals is to draw the rest of humanity inward, making way for them in our intimate circle.[13] He taught that life is a series of concentric circles, the first being the human mind, followed by the circles of immediate family, extended family, local community, neighboring towns, country, and eventually the entire world. This inclusive embrace was known as *oikeiosis* (in Buddhism it's called *metta*, or loving-kindness). We're encouraged to scale the walls of our blockaded lives, to extend our hearts to those closest to us, first, then to acquaintances, strangers, and enemies as our powers of loving-kindness increase. This doesn't imply that we condone bad behavior or sanction their twisted perspectives. We simply drop the conceit (which fuels hatred, violence, and suffering) that *we* are made from different stuff—better, purer, more perfect stuff—than *they are*.

A person cannot fulfill her spiritual potential without taking this crucial step. "One cannot pursue one's own highest good without at the same time necessarily promoting the good of others," Epictetus taught. "Seeking the very best in themselves means actively caring for the welfare of other human beings."[14] Echoing his Stoic forebears, Waldo teaches us to be spiritual grown-ups, to cease denying our interdependence, pick up the tools of self-reliance, and construct a better life for ourselves. We cannot hope to bring healing to the world before this happens. "As we are, so we do; and as we do, so it is done to us. We are the builders of our fortunes" (*W*). In the end, that may be the best news of all.

❧ THE BRIEF ❧

Enlightenment is the goal of human life, and the natural result of knowing yourself. We are wired psychologically for self-realization; the potential for liberation from illusion, ignorance, and self-forgetting is integral to our essential nature. Using reason and self-inquiry to separate the real from the unreal, you increase the ability to see beyond self-image (the me-story) into your authentic Self. This Self is a reflection of the One Mind, both personal and transcendental, an inner giant that's always with you beneath the maelstrom of passing thoughts and feelings. This Self exists only in the eternal present (nunc stans) and can only be experienced in the here and now. You need no outside authority to make this connection, and it's a mistake to look to the past (or tradition) for permission to integrate your interior giant today. If religions continue to glorify the past, downplaying the importance of direct spiritual experience, they fail their essential purpose as bridges to personal enlightenment. For self-reliance to be authentic, it must acknowledge the giant within, which goes by a myriad of names: God, Shakti, Tao, Buddha, Nature, divine intelligence, and so on. Enlarged by awareness of this transcendental Self, you expand the circle of care and compassion, stay aligned with your spiritual origins, and answer the clarion call to self-knowledge for which you were born.

Spiritual Exercises

Emerson and the Stoics were proponents of using spiritual exercises to prompt insight, deepen character, and accelerate well-being. Questions open the doors of perception and sharpen your life skills. It's helpful to take twenty minutes a day, five days a week, to reflect on a spiritual exercise that feels relevant to you. This can be done through personal writing, contemplation, or dialogue with a peer, or in therapy.

Lesson One

Exercise One: Integrate Your Shadow Parts

Reflecting on the law of compensation, consider how you can integrate aspects of your character that you currently conceal due to shame, discomfort, or fear. When you allow your quirks, peculiarities, limitations, and flaws to be part of your character, you flourish.

Deepening Prompt: What aspects of your character do you find unacceptable, and what can you do to integrate them into your awareness? How might this enrich your life? Be specific.

Exercise Two: Don't Be Too Domestic

Reflect on your willingness to be unconventional, spontaneous, and free of exaggerated propriety. Understand that wildness strengthens connection to your body and returns you to your physical nature. This serves to balance the tendency toward headiness, abstraction, emotion-avoidance, and over-domestication.

Deepening Prompt: How would avoiding human-made distractions and secondhand experiences, including addiction to technology, improve your life? Be specific.

Exercise Three: Locate Your Bliss

Examine what brings you joy and purpose, satisfies your soul, and comes most naturally to you. Bliss has more to do with flow and self-realization than with shallow pleasures or momentary satisfactions. Many bliss-inducing endeavors require hard effort and sacrifice.

Deepening Prompt: What brings you joy and purpose—and why—and how do you resist doing the very thing(s) that make you happiest? Be specific.

Lesson Two

Exercise One: Take the View from Above

Imagine yourself from forty thousand feet. Rather than experiencing feelings of insignificance, use this aerial perspective to see yourself in proportion to others and to understand the relative unimportance of what troubles you most. Your greatest challenges, though real, are not what you believe them to be. You are both diminutive and immense.

Deepening Prompt: When you look at your life from forty thousand feet, what is glaringly unimportant that currently causes you anxiety or fear? What makes a new kind of sense?

Exercise Two: Observe Your Responses

Pay serious attention to how you react to people, places, and information coming your direction. Remember to pause, make space for reflection, and ask whether this (fill in the blank) is within your control to change (in which case you should act on it) or isn't (in which case you should know it's not your business). Be mindful of recurring triggers, biases, judgments, fears, and blind spots.

Deepening Prompt: When and with whom are you overly reactive, overinvested, and overemotional, inappropriately, and how do you justify this behavior?

Exercise Three: Learn to Otherize

Reflect on how differently you look at a given event when it happens to you and when it happens to someone else. Notice how much easier it is to remain equanimous when adverse things happen to others, and ask yourself, Why is this so? Try meeting challenges as if they were happening to someone else, and notice the difference.

Deepening Prompt: Imagine a challenge in your life today as if it were happening to a stranger. How does this affect the heaviness of your load?

Lesson Three

Exercise One: Question Your Need to Be Liked

Think about how much time and energy you spend trying to earn other people's approval. Pay attention to how much you censor yourself, adhere to social rules you don't agree with, and fear nonconformity. Seeking permission from others to be yourself is oxymoronic.

Deepening Prompt: When does the need for other people's approval stop you from being authentic, and why do you crave this approval? Be specific.

Exercise Two: Clarify Your Motives

Consider the intentions behind your actions—measure their integrity. Positive actions performed with negative (selfish) intentions are likely to end badly. Notice when you're motivated by fear, desire, reason, aggression, wisdom, or shortsightedness. When you understand what motivates you, skillful action is far more likely.

Deepening Prompt: When in life are your true motivations not in alignment with the results you're seeking? What are the reasons for this contradiction? Be specific.

Exercise Three: Question the Mask of Goodness

Think about what being good means to you, your beliefs about what constitutes goodness, and whether you believe that people are naturally good. Pay attention to the virtue gap between appearance and reality. Avoid virtue signaling and pretense.

Deepening Prompt: Where in your life are you pretending to be better than you are, or "good" in ways that are not authentic?

Lesson Four

Exercise One: Make Space for Paradox

Reflect on the doubleness of experience and how apparent opposites can be equally true at the same time. Remember that there are two sides to what happens, at least, and that wisdom results in the ability to hold opposing truths in your mind at the same time without either canceling the other out. An overarching whole encompasses both, as the circle makes space for yin and yang.

Deepening Prompt: Explore the contradictions and paradoxes of your life and how they fit together to make a whole. How do you fight these paradoxes? Be specific.

Exercise Two: Turn the Obstacle Upside Down

How can you transform adverse conditions into opportunities in your life today? Look at the obstacles you're facing, great and small, through the lens of paradox, and notice how conditions can be optimized by reversing your perspective. Doing so relieves discouragement and reveals new possibilities, workarounds, reversals, shortcuts, and trapdoors to help you get past where you're stuck.

Deepening Prompt: Consider the obstacles in your life today from as many different perspectives as possible. What do you see differently?

Exercise Three: Move Beyond Us-and-Them

Think about the impact of group loyalty in your life. How do tribalism, cliquishness, jingoism, exceptionalism, and group narcissism shape your reality? Notice which personal labels you hold most dear and which you reject. This will help you understand where your enemy-making reactions come from.

Deepening Prompt: What groups do you associate yourself with, and how do these group identities affect your choices, prejudices, and behavior?

Lesson Five

Exercise One: Practice Intentional Choice

Reflect on your own choice-making skills and when you give your power away unnecessarily. Notice how an internal locus of control gives confidence and deepens resilience. No longer a victim of circumstance, you take responsibility for your life and grasp the ability to change course by making different choices.

Deepening Prompt: When and how do you relinquish responsibility for your life and the choices you make by blaming others or outside events? How does this disempower you? Be specific.

Exercise Two: Prepare for Your Day

Consider the uncertainties, disappointments, surprises, and offenses that may befall you on this day. Acknowledging the imperfect nature of things, you can drop unrealistic expectations, knowing that whatever happens, you'll be able to adapt, pivot, and change course. Preparing for likely disappointment is different from pessimism. It's an inoculation of truth to stop yourself from being set up for a fall.

Deepening Prompt: What is most likely to oppose, offend, or distress you in your current life, and how can you prepare yourself to meet disappointment with open eyes?

Exercise Three: Take Things Apart

Think about your attachment to events and people, objects and possessions, and how—when you reduce these things to their smallest parts—your attachment to them changes. When you break externals down to their tiniest constituent parts, you learn to see them for what they are and not place too much value on material things and circumstances. This dispels the magical charm we project onto coveted people, places, and things—as well as the fear of losing them—by revealing them as transitory and conditional.

Deepening Prompt: What do you covet in your life, and how does the object of your covetousness change when you take it apart (e.g., see a beloved pair of shoes as created from the dried skin of dead cows, held together with glue and string, or view a romantic obsession as a flawed human being)?

Lesson Six

Exercise One: Be Instructed by Nature

Reflect on the universal principles at play in nature that shed light on your human experience: the industriousness of the ant and the grace of the falcon, the strength of a redwood, the fluidity of the open sea. As parts of nature, we partake of her virtues. Using your anthropomorphic imagination, allow yourself to be tutored by the creation in its infinite diversity.

Deepening Prompt: Take a journal into nature, quiet your mind, and notice what the biosphere around you is saying. What are the voices of animals, plants, and earth telling you about how to live?

Exercise Two: Locate the Source

Become aware of the aliveness inside you, the flow of energy animating your body and mind. Pay attention to the tingling in your fingertips, the hairs standing up on the back of your neck, the column of vitality in your spine that keeps your skeleton upright. This electric current is your very life force, Dylan Thomas's "force that through the green fuse drives the flower."

Deepening Prompt: When, how, and why do you interfere with maximizing your life force? In what ways do you sabotage your energy and sacrifice your power? Be specific.

Exercise Three: Reflect on Nonduality

Reflect on the unity of all things and the artificial boundaries you place between yourself and the outside world. Recognize these human-made barriers as illusions, and contemplate the indivisible oneness of creation; be mindful that the only thing separating you from unity consciousness is your mind.

Deepening Prompt: How would an awareness of interconnection change your opinions, behaviors, expectations, and struggles with the "outside" world? Be specific.

Lesson Seven

Exercise One: Don't Let Appearances Scare You

Pay attention to being deceived by appearances, which creates unnecessary fear. Remember that fear is irrational, preverbal, and sensitive to stereotypes and that we use mental shorthand to protect ourselves from danger, reacting automatically to scary exteriors whether they pose a real threat or not.

Deepening Prompt: When are you scared off by how things

look even if the truth underneath is far less frightening? Be specific.

Exercise Two: Become Equal to the Task

Inventory areas of your life where you feel incapable of prevailing over obstacles. Pay attention to the stories behind these beliefs, the reality behind your fears. Notice where insufficient preparation or knowledge, shaky self-confidence, and negative predictions stand in your way. Notice when the thought *I can't do this* becomes a refrain, and examine your reasons for believing this.

Deepening Prompt: What do you need to learn, practice, or let go of in order to feel equal to the challenges in your life? Be specific.

Exercise Three: Overcome the Fear of Freedom

Reflect on your anxiety toward the unknown and the fear of acknowledging your own freedom, the multitude of choices before you at any given moment. Notice how this trepidation stops you in your tracks, blaming outside conditions for your paralysis. Freedom is something that many people both crave and resist, like love. We fear greatness and possibility, the unknown in general, and entrap ourselves in low expectations.

Deepening Prompt: How do you define freedom, and when does your fear of freedom interfere with making creative, satisfying choices? Be specific.

Lesson Eight

Exercise One: Choose Your Company Well

Consider the quality of the company you keep, including family, friends, colleagues, and frequent associates. Notice whether these liaisons are elevating or deflating, inspiring or enervating. Ask yourself whether you feel seen, heard, and appreciated by the people you spend your time with; also why, in cases where genuine warmth and affinity are lacking, you stay in these relationships.

Deepening Prompt: Make a list of the people you spend your time with. Evaluate each relationship carefully. In cases where relationships are mandatory (e.g., with family members), how can you optimize these connections and protect yourself from harm? Be specific.

Exercise Two: Learn to Listen

Reflect on the art of listening and on how your ability to listen deeply (or not) affects your close relationships. Become aware that the act of witnessing another person with an open heart and mind is key to feeling empathy; knowing we're seen and heard by people who wish us well is a precious gift, especially in times of struggle.

Deepening Prompt: Are you able to listen closely to others, or are you easily distracted? What interferes with your ability to focus and be present? Be specific.

Exercise Three: Remember Love Is Impersonal

Contemplate love as a universal force, like gravity, that attracts individuals to one another, naturally, in the same way plants reach for the sun. This energy of attraction is identical across all relationships, while the forms of these connections differ. Pay special attention to the ways in which this fact contradicts the myths of romantic love and filial piety, wherein certain kinds of relationships are viewed as more precious than others. Don't mistake the form for the content.

Deepening Prompt: Do your relationships suffer from possessiveness, competition, and fixation on form over content (i.e., the shape of the relationship)? If so, how might they be healed by viewing love as a power, not a possession?

Lesson Nine

Exercise One: Love What Happens

Reflect on the imperfect perfection of your life (*amor fati*) and the rightness of things exactly as they are. When you accept conditions without resistance, you reduce conflict, struggle, and stress. Efforts to improve yourself and your life grow paradoxically more effective when you begin with acceptance. Free of the misconception that something is "wrong" and needs to be fixed, your actions have a more positive and lasting impact.

Deepening Prompt: What conditions in your life do you most resist, and how does this resistance decrease when you practice *amor fati*? Be specific.

Exercise Two: Know That Grief Is Temporary

Reflect on the short life span of emotions and the ever-shifting impacts of pain. Contemplate the truth that pain-plus-story equals suffering, that narratives of loss, blame, and bitterness tend to harden into emotional knots that prevent grief from passing through you.

Deepening Prompt: What are you grieving in your life today, and how do your stories *about* this grief stop it from becoming a thing of the past?

Exercise Three: Consider the Phoenix

Think about the process of resurrection as a natural phase in healing. Notice how life reshapes destruction in unexpected ways, healing wounds believed to be irreparable, instilling vitality where you were lifeless. Pay attention to your phoenix-like capacity to rise with renewed determination from the ashes of what has been lost.

Deepening Prompt: How can you harness the power of resurrection in areas of life where you feel destroyed, knocked down, defeated? Be specific.

Lesson Ten

Exercise One: Practice Realistic Optimism

Pay attention to the regenerative power of hope and how hope buoys the spirit in challenging times. Without ignoring the facts on the ground, how can you optimize your present circumstances? Realize that regardless of what might be happening, *something else is also true.* This realization prompts wakefulness and opens a chink in the wall of the mind to reveal new possibilities.

Deepening Prompt: How can you practice optimism today without denying conditions as they are, and counter the negativity bias? Be specific.

Exercise Two: Stop Judging People and Things

Reflect on the ways you leap to judgment, and notice the effects of your unconscious bias. Practice giving others the benefit of the doubt and pause before casting aspersions on people and things. This can interrupt the destructive judgment-opinion-projection-reaction cycle and reduce the negative impacts of self-fulfilling prophecy.

Deepening Prompt: What and whom do you judge too harshly, and how does this rush to judgment blind you to the truth of people and things? Be specific.

Exercise Three: Lighten Up

Reflect on how you take yourself too seriously. Notice how you exaggerate the importance of your problems, the power of your influence, and the scope and veracity of your pain; and consider how inflated self-importance weighs you down and blocks fresh insight. Self-absorption, rumination, and self-aggrandizement conspire against happiness and can rob your life of gratitude and grace.

Deepening Prompt: In what ways do you take yourself too seriously, and how does this cause you unnecessary suffering? How might your life change if you lightened up? Be specific.

Lesson Eleven

Exercise One: Acknowledge Your Place in the Cosmos

Consider the scale of the cosmos and the vastness of the space in which you exist. Reflect on the innumerable beings in your midst and the forces whose unimaginable power sustain this mysterious creation. Meditating on your place in the cosmos, pay attention to how awe stills the mind, opens the heart, eases conflict, and repairs the illusion of separateness.

Deepening Prompt: When you view your life through this cosmic lens, how does it impact your ability to love and reduce self-pity? Be specific.

Exercise Two: Notice "Lustres" and Epiphanies

Reflect on how to increase your awareness of uncanny, illuminating experiences: transcendent, synchronous moments that open your eyes to a new way of seeing. Consider how epiphanies enlarge your being and reveal the extraordinary nature of ordinary things.

Deepening Prompt: Describe an epiphany or peak experience that changed your perception of reality in as much detail as possible. What did you learn from this moment? Be specific.

Exercise Three: Look Through the Eyes of Love

Reflect on your existence through a lens of unconditional care and affection, bringing gratitude, tenderness, tolerance, and wonder to how you see. Imagine your life through the eyes of God (or unity consciousness), and notice the miraculous dimension of being, the fragility and impermanence of creation, and how perspective elevates your heart and mind.

Deepening Prompt: When you view your daily life through the eyes of love, what becomes obvious that escapes your attention otherwise? Be specific.

Lesson Twelve

Exercise One: Let Go of the Past

Reflect on how you can let go of the past by building present moment awareness. Know that every moment is a new beginning and that what has happened is dead and gone. Don't be a slave to history and tradition, and practice not investing past achievements or failures with exaggerated importance. Know that existence is seen as an ongoing act of creation whose power is found in the present moment.

Deepening Prompt: How are you controlled by the past, revering the achievements of predecessors at the expense of your own self-belief? Be specific.

Exercise Two: Practice Rational Transcendence

Think about how you can integrate reason into your spiritual life. Know that the conflict between transcendental awareness and rationality is a figment of the imagination. When you look closely at this polarizing, materialistic perspective, it crumbles to pieces. Remember that the physical and spiritual, personal and transpersonal, visible and invisible, are aspects of the same indivisible whole.

Deepening Prompt: When does reason interfere with your spiritual awareness, and vice versa? Be specific.

Exercise Three: Expand the Circle

Consider how to enlarge your range of compassion and expand your field of loving-kindness to include all of humankind. Notice where your heart closes, becomes numb, and excludes other people from the circle of care. Pay special attention to your aversion-triggers and to when you shrink away from fellow-feeling toward others whom you distance or demonize.

Deepening Prompt: Explore which groups and individuals you exclude from your circle of compassion, how self-distancing diminishes you as a person, and how you can begin to humanize the "other" as deserving of your fellow-feeling.

ACKNOWLEDGMENTS

My deepest thanks to Dr. Barbara Packer for introducing me to Emerson, and to my beloved agent Joy Harris for shepherding this book into the world with great patience.

I'm grateful to Mickey Maudlin, whose astute notes greatly improved the manuscript, and to Gideon Weil and Chantal Tom for their enthusiasm and love of Emerson's work. Without the research and editorial assistance of Marybeth Hamilton, Rena Graham, and Sharyl Volpe, this book might never have seen the light of day, and to friends and colleagues who supported me through the years of writing, my deepest thanks: Barbara Graham, Florence Falk, Lisa Kentgen, Martha Cooley, V, Celeste Lecesne, Hugh Delehanty, Naomi Shragai, Gary Lennon, Trisha Coburn, Joe Dolce, Mercedes Ruehl, Gwenyth Jackaway, Eve Eliot, Kate Rabinowitz, and Karen Fuchs. Also, deep bows to Lynn Whittemore and Doug Goodman for offering a quiet place to work in Cambridge when I needed it.

I'm also deeply indebted to the Emerson scholars whose work inspired me during this writing, particularly Robert Richardson, Joel Porte, Carl Bode, Carlos Baker, Van Wyck Brooks, and Gay Wilson Allen.

Thanks to Francis Bok, Trisha Coburn, Patricia Carew, Andrea Martin, Adisa Krupalija, John Dugdale, and those students who allowed me to use their stories to illustrate the power and possibilities of self-reliance.

Most of all, enormous gratitude to David Moore, my best friend and partner in all things.

NOTES

Preface

1. Ralph Waldo Emerson, *Journals and Miscellaneous Notebooks of Ralph Waldo Emerson*, vol. 3: *1826–1832*, eds. William Gilman and Alfred R. Ferguson (Cambridge: Harvard Univ. Press, 1963).

2. Ralph Waldo Emerson, *Emerson in His Journals*, ed. Joel Porte (Cambridge: Belknap Press of Harvard Univ. Press, 1982), 206.

3. Lucius Annaeus Seneca, *Letters on Ethics: To Lucilius*, trans. Margaret Graver and A. A. Long (Chicago: Univ. of Chicago Press, 2015), 14.

INTRODUCTION
Trust Yourself

1. Joel Lovell, "George Saunders's Advice to Graduates," *The New York Times: The 6th Floor Blog*, July 2013, https://archive.nytimes.com/6thfloor.blogs.nytimes.com/2013/07/31/george-saunderss-advice-to-graduates/.

2. Gay Wilson Allen, *Waldo Emerson: A Biography* (New York: Viking Press, 1981), 147.

3. John Townsend Trowbridge, "Reminiscences of Walt Whitman," *The Atlantic*, February 1902.

4. Sarah Bakewell, *How to Live: Or a Life of Montaigne in One Question and Twenty Attempts at an Answer* (New York: Other Press, 2011).

5. W. E. B. Du Bois, *The Souls of Black Folk* (Aurora, CO: Chump Change, 1903).

6. Robert D. Richardson Jr., *Emerson: The Mind on Fire* (Berkeley: Univ. of California Press, 1995), 571.

7. Ralph Waldo Emerson, *The Topical Notebooks of Ralph Waldo Emerson*, vol. 3, ed. Ralph H. Orth and Glen M. Johnson (Columbia, MO: Univ. of Missouri Press, 1994), 76.

8. Alia E. Dastagir, "More Young People Are Dying by Suicide, and Experts Aren't Sure Why," *USA Today,* September 2020, https://www.usatoday.com/story/news/health/2020/09/11/youth-suicide-rate-increases-cdc-report-finds/3463549001/.

9. Emily Baumgaertner, "How Many Teenage Girls Deliberately Harm Themselves? Nearly 1 in 4, Survey Finds," *New York Times*, July 2, 2018, https://www.nytimes.com/2018/07/02/health/self-harm-teenagers-cdc.html.

10. "Stress in America: Money, Inflation, War Pile on to Nation Stuck in COVID-19 Survival Mode," American Psychological Association, March 2022, https://www.apa.org/news/press/releases/stress/2022/march-2022-survival-mode?utm_source=twitter&utm_medium=social&utm_campaign=apa-stress&utm_content=sia-mar22-money#inflation.

11. Mary Oliver, *Upstream: Selected Essays* (New York: Penguin, 2016).

12. "In U.S., Decline of Christianity Continues at Rapid Pace," Pew Research Center, October 17, 2019, https://www.pewresearch.org/religion/2019/10/17/in-u-s-decline-of-christianity-continues-at-rapid-pace/.

13. Dr. Miklos Hargitay, "Stoicism: The Philosophical Roots of Cognitive Behavioral Therapy," *Manhattan Therapy Collective Blog* (November 2020).

LESSON ONE
On Originality: Character Is Everything

1. Van Wyck Brooks, *The Life of Emerson* (New York: E. P. Dutton, 1932).

2. Ralph Waldo Emerson, *The Selected Letters of Ralph Waldo Emerson*, ed. Joel Myerson (New York: Columbia Univ. Press, 1998), 68.

3. Ralph Waldo Emerson, *Complete Works with a Biographical Introduction and Notes by Edward Waldo Emerson, and a General Index*, vol. 10 (Boulder: Univ. of Colorado, Boulder, 1911), 407.

4. Ralph Waldo Emerson, *Selected Writings of Ralph Waldo Emerson* (New York: W. Scott, 1888), xii.

5. Ralph Waldo Emerson, *The Heart of Emerson's Journals*, ed. Bliss Perry (Wentworth Press, 2019), 39.

6. James Woelfel, "Emerson and the Stoic Tradition," *American Journal of Theology and Philosophy* 32, no. 2 (May 2011), 122.

7. Buckminster Fuller, *Utopia or Oblivion: The Prospects for Humanity* (New York: Penguin, 1972), 62.

8. Emerson, *The Selected Letters*, 306.

9. Satu Teerikangas and Liisa Välikangas, "Exploring the Dynamic of Evoking Intuition," *Handbook of Research Methods on Intuition* (London: Edgar Elgar Publishing, 2014), 72–78.

10. Ralph Waldo Emerson, *Emerson in His Journals*, ed. Joel Porte (Cambridge: Belknap Press of Harvard Univ. Press, 1982), 71.

11. Emerson, *Emerson in His Journals*, 199.

12. Mike Yarbrough, "The Mind of Man: Compartmentalization," *Wolf & Iron: Feed the Wolf, Be the Iron* (n.d.), https://wolfandiron.com /blogs/feedthewolf/the-mind-of-a-man-compartmentalization.

13. Alexandra Mysoor, "The Science Behind Intuition and How You Can Use It to Get Ahead at Work," *Forbes*, February 2017, https://www .forbes.com/sites/alexandramysoor/2017/02/02/the-science-behind -intuition-and-how-you-can-use-it-to-get-ahead-at-work/?sh=4e3895b8239f.

14. Joel Porte and Saundra Morris, eds., *The Cambridge Companion to Ralph Waldo Emerson* (Cambridge, UK: Cambridge Univ. Press, 1999), 41.

15. Andy Warhol, *The Philosophy of Andy Warhol* (San Diego: Harcourt, 1975), 149.

16. Lawrence Buell, *Emerson* (Cambridge: Harvard Univ. Press, 2003), 73.

17. Erich Fromm, *The Sane Society* (New York: Rinehart, 1955), 25.

18. Erich Fromm and Leonard A. Anderson, *The Sane Society* (Abingdon, UK: Taylor & Francis, 2017), xxvi.

19. Amanda L. Chan, "6 Unexpected Ways Writing Can Transform Your Health," *HuffPost*, December 6, 2017, https://www.huffpost.com /entry/writing-health-benefits-journal_n_4242456.

20. Stephen Dunn, "A Secret Life," A Cottage by the Sea, September 11, 2015, https://www.acottagebythesea.net/poems/a -secret-life-by-stephen-dunn.

21. Lord Byron, *The Works of Lord Byron* (Palala Press, 2015).

22. Jayne O'Donnell, "Teens Aren't Socializing in the Real World. And That's Making Them Super Lonely," *USA Today*, March 20, 2019, https://www.usatoday.com/story/news/health/2019/03/20/teen -loneliness-social-media-cell-phones-suicide-isolation-gaming-cigna /3208845002/.

23. O'Donnell, "Teens Aren't Socializing."

24. Ian Sample, "Shocking but True: Students Prefer Jolt of Pain to Being Made to Sit and Think," *The Guardian*, July 3, 2014, https://www .theguardian.com/science/2014/jul/03/electric-shock-preferable-to -thinking-says-study.

25. D. W. Winnicott, "The Capacity to Be Alone," *The International Journal of Psychoanalysis* 39 (September 1958), 416–20.

26. C. G. Jung, Herbert Read, Gerhard Adler, and Michael Fordham, *Collected Works of C.G. Jung,* vol. 13: *Alchemical Studies* (Princeton, NJ: Princeton Univ. Press, 1953), 265.

27. Howard Thurman, *Meditations of the Heart* (Boston: Beacon Press, 2014), 92.

LESSON TWO
On Perspective: You Are How You See

1. Evan Puschak, *Escape into Meaning: Essays on Superman, Public Benches, and Other Obsessions* (New York: Atria Books, 2022), 20.

2. Ralph Waldo Emerson, *Journals of Ralph Waldo Emerson: With Annotations*, vol. 3, ed. Edward Waldo Emerson and Waldo Emerson Forbes (Reprint Services Corporation, 2008), 272.

3. Bessel van der Kolk, *The Body Keeps the Score: Brain, Mind, and Body in the Healing of Trauma* (New York: Viking, 2014), 191.

4. John M. de Castro, "Different Meditation Types Alter Brain Connectivity Patterns Differently Over the Long Term," Contemplative Studies, November 2021, http://contemplative-studies.org/wp/index .php/2021/11/24/different-meditation-types-alter-brain-connectivity -patters-differently-over-the-long-term/.

5. Lou E. Whitaker, "How Does Thinking Positive Thoughts Affect Neuroplasticity?," Meteor Education: Accelerating Engagement, n.d., https://meteoreducation.com/how-does-thinking-positive-thoughts -affect-neuroplasticity/.

6. Buddha, *Dhammapada*, a collection of sayings of the Buddha in verse form and one of the most widely read and best-known Buddhist scriptures.

7. "What Is the Default Mode Network?," *Psychology Today*, n.d., https://www.psychologytoday.com/us/basics/default-mode-network.

8. Marcus Aurelius, *Meditations: A New Translation*, trans. Gregory Hays (New York: Random House, 2002), 59.

9. Amanda L. Chan, "6 Unexpected Ways Writing Can Transform Your Health," *HuffPost*, updated December 2, 2017, https://www .huffpost.com/entry/writing-health-benefits-journal_n_4242456.

10. James Pennebaker, "Writing About Emotional Experiences as a Therapeutic Process," *Psychological Science* 8, no. 3 (May 1997), 162–66.

11. This is a basic tenet of Victor Frankl's "Logotherapy."

12. Jerry Mayer and John P. Holms, comps., *Bite-Size Einstein:*

Quotations on Just About Everything from the Greatest Mind of the Twentieth Century (New York: St. Martin's Publishing Group, 2015).

13.　Jonathan Haidt, *The Happiness Hypothesis: Finding Modern Truth in Ancient Wisdom* (New York: Basic Books, 2006), 13.

14.　Ralph Waldo Emerson, *Emerson in His Journals*, ed. Joel Porte (Cambridge: Belknap Press of Harvard Univ. Press, 1982).

15.　Steve Bradt, "Wandering Mind Not a Happy Mind," *Harvard Gazette*, November 11, 2010.

16.　Matthew A. Killingsworth and Daniel T. Gilbert, Harvard Univ. study, published in *Science Daily*, November 12, 2010.

LESSON THREE
On Nonconformity: Build Your Own World

1.　Marcus Aurelius, *Meditations: A New Translation*, trans. Gregory Hays (New York: Random House, 2002), 32.

2.　Ralph Waldo Emerson, *Emerson in His Journals*, ed. Joel Porte (Cambridge: Belknap Press of Harvard Univ. Press, 1982).

3.　Harold Bloom and Luca Prono, eds., *Henry David Thoreau* (Facts on File, 2014), 21.

4.　Bloom and Prono, eds., *Henry David Thoreau*, 102.

5.　Ralph Waldo Emerson, *Emerson's Complete Works*, Riverside ed., vol. 2, ed. Edward Waldo Emerson and James Elliot Cabot (digitized, 2007), 102.

6.　Alfred I. Tauber, *Henry David Thoreau and the Moral Agency of Knowing* (Berkeley: Univ. of California Press, 2003), 25.

7.　Frances Eggleston Blodgett and Andrew Burr Blodgett, *The Blodgett Readers by Grades, Book 6* (Boston: Ginn and Co., 1910), 116.

8.　Emerson, *Emerson in His Journals*, 181.

9.　Henry David Thoreau, *Walden: A Fully Annotated Edition* (New Haven, CT: Yale Univ. Press, 2004), 92.

10.　Eldad Yechiam, "The Psychology of Gains and Losses: More Complicated Than Previously Thought," *American Psychological*

Association, January 2015, https://www.apa.org/science/about/psa /2015/01/gains-losses.

11. Saul Mcleod, "Asch Conformity Line Experiment," Simply Psychology, February 2, 2023, https://simplypsychology.org/asch -conformity.html.

12. Al Christensen, "Nomad Origin Stories: Joe," January 17, 2017, https://youtu.be/TiuI2FZSMzs (3:55).

13. Dan Ariely, *Predictably Irrational: The Hidden Forces That Shape Our Decisions* (New York: Harper, 2009).

14. Richard Joyce, *Evolution of Morality* (Cambridge: MIT Press, 2007), 110.

15. William Wordsworth, *The Complete Poetical Works of William Wordsworth* (Philadelphia: Troutman & Hayes, 2008), 85.

16. E. E. Cummings, *E. E. Cummings Complete Poems, 1904–1962* (New York: Liveright, 1994).

17. Colin Wilson, *The Ultimate Colin Wilson: Writings on Mysticism, Consciousness and Existentialism*, ed. Colin Stanley (London: Watkins Media, 2019).

18. Andrew Harvey and Mark Matousek, *Dialogues with a Modern Mystic* (Wheaton, IL: Theosophical Publishing House, 1994), 33.

19. Epictetus, *The Art of Living* (Prabhat Prakashan, 2021).

20. Ralph Waldo Emerson, *Journals*, vol. 7, ed. Edward Waldo Emerson and Waldo Emerson Forbes (Bibliography Center for Research, 2009), 407.

21. Ralph Waldo Emerson, *Complete Works of Ralph Waldo Emerson, Illustrated: Nature, Self-Reliance, Experience, The Poet, The Over-Soul, Circles* (Strelbytskyy Multimedia Publishing, 2021).

22. Ralph Waldo Emerson, *Self-Reliance: The Unparalleled Vision of Personal Power*, ed. Mitch Horowitz (New York: Gildan Media, 2018).

23. Robert Lawson-Peebles, *American Literature Before 1880* (London: Taylor & Francis, 2003), 188.

LESSON FOUR

On Contradiction: Everything Is Double

1. Kaiping Peng and Richard E. Nisbett, "Culture, Dialectics, and Reasoning About Contradiction," Univ. of California at Berkeley/Univ. of Michigan, n.d., http://www-personal.umich.edu/~nisbett/cultdialectics.pdf.

2. Martin Buber, *I and Thou* (Marlborough, MA: eBookit.com, 2012).

3. Frans de Waal, *Primates and Philosophers: How Morality Evolved* (Princeton, NJ: Princeton Univ. Press, 2006), 155.

4. Lawrence Wilde, *Erich Fromm and the Quest for Solidarity* (New York: Palgrave Macmillan US, 2016), 134.

5. Robert Gooding-Williams, *In the Shadow of Du Bois: Afro-Modern Political Thought in America* (Cambridge: Harvard Univ. Press, 2011).

6. Lance Morrow, *Evil: An Investigation*, trans. Gregory Hays (New York: Basic Books, 2003), 25.

7. Marcus Aurelius, *Meditations: A New Translation*, trans. Gregory Hayes (New York: Random House, 2002), 34.

8. Ralph Waldo Emerson, *The American Scholar: Self-Reliance, Compensation* (Woodstock, GA: American Book, 1893), 105.

9. Ralph Waldo Emerson, *Journals and Miscellaneous Notebooks of Ralph Waldo Emerson,* vol. 1: *1819–1822,* ed. William H. Gilman, Alfred R. Ferguson, George P. Clark, and Merrell R. Davis (Cambridge: Belknap Press of Harvard Univ. Press, 1974), 133.

10. Emerson, *Journals and Miscellaneous Notebooks,* vol. 1, 39.

11. Marcus Aurelius, *Meditations,* 41.

12. Ralph Waldo Emerson, *Journals,* vol. 8 (Wentworth Press, 2016), 380.

13. George Kateb, *Emerson and Self-Reliance* (Lanham, MD: Rowman & Littlefield, 2002), 123.

14. Margaret Fuller, *The Essential Margaret Fuller*, ed. Jeffrey Steele (Princeton, NJ: Rutgers Univ. Press, 1994), xxxiv.

15. Kate Bornstein, "Naming All the Parts," The Middlebury Blog Network, 2013, http://sites.middlebury.edu.

LESSON FIVE
On Resilience: Without Confidence, the Universe Is Against You

1. Courtney E. Ackerman, "What Is Self-Efficacy Theory? (Incl. 8 Examples & Scales)," *Positive Psychology*, May 29, 2018, https://positive psychology.com/self-efficacy/.

2. Robert Holman Coombs, *Addiction Counseling Review: Preparing for Comprehensive, Certification, and Licensing Examinations* (London: Taylor & Francis, 2004), 77.

3. Maurice York and Rick Spaulding, *Ralph Waldo Emerson: The Infinitude of the Private Man* (Ann Arbor, MI: Wrightwood Press, 2008), 20.

4. Ralph Waldo Emerson, *The Letters of Ralph Waldo Emerson*, vol. 4, ed. Ralph L. Rusk (New York: Columbia Univ. Press, 1939), 439.

5. Michael Lounsbury, Nelson Phillips, and Paul Tracey, *Religion and Organization Theory* (Bradford, UK: Emerald Group Publishing, 2014), 138.

6. Marcus Tullius Cicero, *On the Nature of the Gods: On Divination; On Fate; On the Republic; On the Laws; and On Standing for the Consulship* (Urbana-Champaign: Univ. of Illinois at Urbana-Champaign, 1902).

7. Lucius Annaeus Seneca, *Fifty Letters of a Roman Stoic*, trans. Margaret Graver and A. A. Long (Chicago: Univ. of Chicago Press, 2021), 35.

8. P. Gollwitzer, "Implementation Intentions: Strong Effects of Simple Plans," *American Psychologist*, July 1, 1999.

9. Brené Brown, *Daring Greatly: How the Courage to Be Vulnerable Transforms the Way We Live, Love, Parent, and Lead* (New York: Penguin, 2013).

LESSON SIX

On Vitality: A Stream of Power Runs Through You

1. Dominique Mann, "After Every Trauma I've Faced as a Black Woman, I've Turned to the Woods," *Glamour*, February 2021, https://www.glamour.com/story/after-every-trauma-ive-faced-as-a -black-woman-ive-turned-to-the-woods.

2. Andreas Weber, *Matter and Desire: An Erotic Ecology* (White River Junction, VT: Green Publishing, 2017), 135.

3. Mukul Sharma, "Quantum Interconnectedness," *Economic Times*, March 20, 2009.

4. Jalal Al Rumi, *The Essential Rumi*, trans. Coleman Barks (San Francisco: HarperOne, 2004).

5. Louise Gilder, *The Age of Entanglement: When Quantum Physics Was Reborn* (New York: Vintage Books, 2009).

6. Fyodor Dostoyevsky, *The Idiot: A Novel in Four Parts* (London: Heinemann, 1916), 383.

7. Marcus Aurelius, *Meditations: A New Translation*, trans. Gregory Hays (New York: Random House, 2002).

8. Ryan Holiday and Stephen Hanselman, *The Daily Stoic: 366 Meditations on Wisdom, Perseverance, and the Art of Living* (New York: Penguin, 2016).

9. Walter Isaacson, *Steve Jobs* (New York: Simon & Schuster, 2013), 82.

10. Epictetus, *The Complete Works: Handbook, Discourses, and Fragments*, ed. and trans. Robin Waterfield (Chicago: Univ. of Chicago Press, 2022), 55.

11. Peter Y. Chou, ed. "One Universal Mind," WisdomPortal.com, May 26, 1837.

LESSON SEVEN
On Courage: The Death of Fear

1. Mary Oliver, *Upstream: Selected Essays* (New York: Penguin, 2016).

2. Robert Richardson Jr., *Emerson: The Mind on Fire* (Berkeley: Univ. of California Press, 1995), 179.

3. Haiku by Mizuta Masahide, as noted in David Brother Steindl-Rast, *i am through you so I* (Mahwah, NJ: Paulist Press, 2017).

4. Eric Lindberg, "Veteran and Firefighter Who Saved Countless Lives Struggled to Save His Own," USC Trojan Family, winter 2021, https://news.usc.edu/trojan-family/michael-washington-marine-veteran-firefighter-social-work-trauma-hope-healing

5. Ralph Waldo Emerson, *Everyday Emerson: A Year of Wisdom* (New York: St. Martin's, 2022), 25.

6. Evgenia Cherkasova, *Dostoevsky and Kant: Dialogues on Ethics* (Amsterdam: Rodopi, 2009), 73.

7. Ralph Waldo Emerson, *Society and Solitude: Twelve Chapters* (London: S. Low, Son & Marston, 2006), 227.

8. Claudia Deane, Kim Parker, and John Gramlich, "A Year of U.S. Public Opinion on the Coronavirus Pandemic," Pew Research Center, March 5, 2021, https://www.pewresearch.org/2021/03/05/a-year-of-u-s-public-opinion-on-the-coronavirus-pandemic/.

9. A. N. Schelle, "Social Atrophy: Failure in the Flesh," Indiana University South Bend, April 2013, https://clas.iusb.edu/search/?q=Schelle.

10. David Robson, "The Threat of Contagion Can Twist Our Psychological Responses to Ordinary Interactions, Leading Us to Behave in Unexpected Ways," BBC Future, April 2, 2020: 3. https://www.counsellingresources.co.nz/uploads/3/9/8/5/3985535/fear_of_coronavirus_is_changing_our_psychology.pdf.

11. Grenville Kleiser, *Dictionary of Proverbs* (APH Publishing, 2005).

12. Ralph Waldo Emerson, *Journals and Miscellaneous Notebooks of Ralph Waldo Emerson*, vol. 8: *1841–1843*, ed. William H. Gilman

and J. E. Parsons (Cambridge: Belknap Press of Harvard Univ. Press, 1960), 60.

13. Wilhelm Reich, *The Mass Psychology of Fascism*, 3rd ed. (New York: Farrar, Straus and Giroux, 2013).

14. Frederick Douglass, *Narrative of the Life of Frederick Douglass* (Mineola, NY: Dover Publications, 1995), 73.

LESSON EIGHT
On Intimacy: Love Is the Masterpiece of Nature

1. Ralph Waldo Emerson, *Complete Works of Ralph Waldo Emerson, Illustrated: Nature, Self-Reliance, Experience, The Poet, The Over-Soul, Circles* (Strelbytskyy Multimedia Publishing, 2021).

2. Larry A. Carlson, "Bronson Alcott's 'Journal for 1837' (part two)," *Studies in the American Renaissance* (1982): 53–167, https://www .jstor.org/stable/30227495.

3. Ralph Waldo Emerson, *Emerson in His Journals*, ed. Joel Porte (Cambridge: Belknap Press of Harvard Univ. Press, 1982), 230.

4. Ralph Waldo Emerson, *The Heart of Emerson's Journals*, ed. Bliss Perry (Wentworth Press, 2019), 123.

5. Margaret Fuller Ossoli, *Life Without and Life Within* (Outlook Verlag, 2020), 70.

6. Ralph Waldo Emerson, *Journals and Miscellaneous Notebooks of Ralph Waldo Emerson*, vol. 8: *1841–1843*, ed. William H. Gilman and J. E. Parsons (Cambridge: Belknap Press of Harvard Univ. Press, 1960), 34.

7. Rainer Maria Rilke, *Rilke on Love and Other Difficulties: Translations and Considerations*, trans. John J. L. Mood (New York: W. W. Norton, 1994), 45.

8. Emerson, *Journals and Miscellaneous Notebooks*, vol. 8, 34.

9. Emerson, *The Heart of Emerson's Journals*, 129.

10. Ralph Waldo Emerson, *The Selected Letters of Ralph Waldo Emerson*, ed. Joel Myerson (New York: Columbia Univ. Press, 1997), 228.

11. Ralph Waldo Emerson, *Journals and Miscellaneous Notebooks of Ralph Waldo Emerson*, vol. 5: *1835–1838*, ed. William Gilman and Alfred R. Ferguson (Cambridge: Harvard Univ. Press, 1965), 336.

12. Emerson, *Emerson in His Journals*, 264.

13. Margaret Fuller, *The Woman and the Myth: Margaret Fuller's Life and Writings*, ed. Bell Gale Chevigny (Boston: Northeastern Univ. Press, 1976), 124.

14. Emerson, *The Selected Letters*, 223.

15. Emerson, *Emerson in His Journals*, 414.

16. John Keats, "Letter to Benjamin Bailey," n.d., http://www.john-keats.com/briefe/221117.htm.

17. Giannis Stamatellos, *Plotinus and the Presocratics: A Philosophical Study of Presocratic Influences in Plotinus' Enneads* (New York: State Univ. of New York Press, 2012), 104.

18. Marcus Aurelius, *Meditations: A New Translation*, trans. Gregory Hays (New York: Random House, 2002), 56.

LESSON NINE

On Adversity: When It Is Dark Enough, You Can See the Stars

1. Theodore Roethke, *On Poetry and Craft: Selected Prose* (Port Townsend, WA: Copper Canyon Press, 2013), 11.

2. Marcus Aurelius, *Meditations: A New Translation*, trans. Gregory Hays (New York: Random House, 2002), 17.

3. Edwin John Ellis and William Butler Yeats, eds., *The Works of William Blake: Poetic, Symbolic, and Critical* (Ann Arbor: Univ. of Michigan, 1893), 432.

4. Lucius Annaeus Seneca, *Dialogues and Essays*, trans. John Davie (Oxford: Oxford Univ. Press, 2008), 64.

5. Marcus Aurelius, Epictetus, and Lucius Annaeus Seneca, *Stoic Six Pack: Meditations of Marcus Aurelius, The Golden Sayings, Fragments and Discourses of Epictetus, Letters from a Stoic, and The Enchiridion*, trans. Gregory Long (Lulu, 2015), 421.

6. Amy Morin, "7 Scientifically Proven Benefits of Gratitude That Will Motivate You to Give Thanks Year-Round," *Forbes*, November 23, 2014, https://www.forbes.com/sites/amymorin/2014/11/23/7 -scientifically-proven-benefits-of-gratitude-that-will-motivate-you-to -give-thanks-year-round/?sh=6c33e72f183c.

7. Derek Beres, "How to Raise a Non-materialistic Kid," Big Think, October 22, 2018, https://bigthink.com/neuropsych/how-can -i-make-my-kid-less-materialistic/.

8. Marcus Tullius Cicero, *Catilinarian Orations from the Text of Ernesti* (Longman, 1829), xxxi.

9. Ralph Waldo Emerson, *Journals and Miscellaneous Notebooks of Ralph Waldo Emerson*, vol. 8: *1841–1843*, ed. William H. Gilman and J. E. Parsons (Cambridge: Belknap Press of Harvard Univ. Press, 1970).

10. Ralph Waldo Emerson, *The Letters of Ralph Waldo Emerson*, vol. 7: *1807–1844*, ed. Eleanor Marguerite Tilton (New York: Columbia Univ. Press, 1939), 502.

11. Courtney E. Ackerman, "Dabrowski's Theory of Positive Disintegration in Psychology," *Positive Psychology*, August 4, 2017, https://positivepsychology.com/dabrowskis-positive-disintegration/.

LESSON TEN
On Optimism: The Soul Refuses Limits

1. Ralph Waldo Emerson, *The Poems of Ralph Waldo Emerson* (Boston: Houghton Mifflin, 1904).

2. John Dewey and Patricia R. Baysinger, *The Middle Works, 1899– 1924* (Carbondale: Southern Illinois Univ. Press, 1997), 191.

3. Marcus Aurelius, *Meditations: A New Translation*, trans. Gregory Hays (New York: Random House, 2002), 113.

4. William James, *Pragmatism and Other Writings* (New York: Penguin, 2000), 312.

5. Kate Bowler, *Blessed: A History of the American Prosperity Gospel* (Oxford: Oxford Univ. Press, 2013).

6. Kate Bowler, "Death, the Prosperity Gospel and Me," *New York Times*, February 14, 2016, https://www.nytimes.com/2016/02/14 /opinion/sunday/death-the-prosperity-gospel-and-me.html.

7. William James, *Essays, Comments, and Reviews* (Cambridge: Harvard Univ. Press, 1987), 310.

8. Anne Trafton, "How Expectation Influences Perception," MIT News, July 15, 2019, https://news.mit.edu/2019/how-expectation -influences-perception-0715.

9. Jerome Groopman, *The Anatomy of Hope: How People Prevail in the Face of Illness* (New York: Random House, 2003).

10. James Bond Stockdale, *Courage Under Fire: Testing Epictetus's Doctrines in a Laboratory of Human Behavior* (Stanford, CA: Hoover Institution Press, 2013).

11. Rabindranath Tagore, *The Complete Works: Poems, Novels, Short Stories, Plays, Essays & Lectures* (DigiCat, 2022), ccclvii.

12. Tali Sharot, "With Age Comes Unbridled Optimism," *Tampa Bay Times*, January 21, 2013, https://www.tampabay.com/news/aging /lifetimes/with-age-comes-unbridled-optimism/1271646/.

13. Martin Luther King Jr., *The Radical King*, ed. Cornel West (Boston: Beacon Press, 2016), 79.

14. Marcus Aurelius, *Meditations*, 151.

15. Marcus Aurelius, *Meditations*, 110.

16. Henry David Thoreau, *Letters to Various Persons* (Boston: Ticknor and Fields, 1865), 46.

LESSON ELEVEN
On Awe: The Proper Emotion Is Wonder

1. John Muir, *Cruise of the Revenue-Steamer Corwin in Alaska and the N.W. Arctic Ocean in 1881: Botanical Notes: Notes and Memoranda: Medical and Anthropological; Botanical; Ornithological* (Creative Media Partners, 2015).

2. John Muir, *Delphi Complete Works of John Muir, Illustrated* (Delphi, 2017).

3. John Muir, *John Muir: His Life and Letters and Other Writings* (Bâton Wicks, 1996), 132.

4. John Muir, Letter from Muir to Emerson, March 18, 1872 (Online Archive of California).

5. Peter James Holliday, *American Arcadia: California and the Classical Tradition* (Oxford: Oxford Univ. Press, 2013), 3.

6. Ralph Waldo Emerson, *Journals and Miscellaneous Notebooks of Ralph Waldo Emerson*, vol. 2: *1822–1826*, ed. William H. Gilman, Alfred R. Ferguson, and Merrell R. Davis (Cambridge: Belknap Press of Harvard Univ. Press, 1961), 116.

7. Robert D. Richardson Jr., *Emerson: The Mind on Fire* (Berkeley: Univ. of California Press, 1995), 5.

8. Abraham H. Maslow, *Religions, Values, and Peak-Experiences* (BN Publishing, 2019).

9. Abraham H. Maslow, *Toward a Psychology of Being* (New York: Wiley, 1999), 118.

10. Abraham Harold Maslow, Robert Frager, Ruth Cox, and James Fadiman, *Motivation and Personality* (New York: Harper and Row, 1987), 160.

11. Jean Grasso Fitzpatrick, *Something More: Nurturing Your Child's Spiritual Growth* (New York: Penguin, 1992), 35.

12. Ralph Waldo Emerson, *Emerson in His Journals*, ed. Joel Porte (Cambridge: Belknap Press of Harvard Univ. Press, 1982), 122.

13. Emily Mae Mentock, "Why 'Awe' Might Be the Secret Ingredient for Happiness," Grotto, n.d., https://grottonetwork.com/navigate-life/health-and-wellness/why-wonder-and-awe-can-lead-to-a-happier-life/.

14. Victor M. Parachin, *Eleven Modern Mystics and the Secrets of a Happy, Holy Life* (Hope Publishing House, 2011), 1.

15. Maslow, *Toward a Psychology of Being*.

16. Nathaniel Hawthorne, *The Complete Works of Nathaniel Hawthorne* (Strelbytskyy Multimedia Publishing, 2022).

17. George Santayana, *Selected Critical Writings of George Santayana*, ed. Norman Henfrey (Cambridge, UK: Cambridge Univ. Press, 1968), 117.

18. Abraham Joshua Heschel, *God in Search of Man: A Philosophy of Judaism* (New York: Farrar, Straus and Giroux, 1976), 112.

19. T. S. Eliot, "Vergil and the Christian World," *The Sewanee Review* 61, no. 1 (1953): 1–14.

20. James Joyce, *Dubliners* (New York: Knopf, 1991), xxiv.

21. Evelyn Underhill, *Mysticism: A Study in Nature and Development of Spiritual Consciousness* (Devoted Publishing, 2017), 8.

22. Frederick Buechner, *Beyond Words: Daily Readings in the ABC's of Faith* (New York: HarperCollins, 2009), 268.

23. Abraham H. Maslow, *Religions, Values, and Peak-Experiences* (Rare Treasure Editions, 2021), viii.

24. Maslow, *Toward a Psychology of Being*.

LESSON TWELVE
On Enlightenment:
Your Giant Goes with You Wherever You Go

1. Aldous Huxley, *The Perennial Philosophy: An Interpretation of the Great Mystics, East and West* (New York: HarperCollins, 2012).

2. Huxley, *The Perennial Philosophy*, 14.

3. Jonathan Haidt, *The Happiness Hypothesis: Finding Modern Truth in Ancient Wisdom* (New York: Basic Books, 2006).

4. Nitin Mishra, *The Diary of a Yogi* (Chennai, India: Notion Press, 1921).

5. Michael Lipka and Claire Gecewicz, "More Americans Now Say They're Spiritual but Not Religious," Pew Research Center, September 6, 2017, https://www.pewresearch.org/fact-tank/2017/09/06/more-americans-now-say-theyre-spiritual-but-not-religious/.

6. Ralph Waldo Emerson, *The Letters of Ralph Waldo Emerson*, vol. 7: *1807–1844*, ed. Eleanor Marguerite Tilton (New York: Columbia Univ. Press, 1939), 7.

7. Ralph Waldo Emerson, *Journals and Miscellaneous Notebooks of Ralph Waldo Emerson*, vol. 2: *1822–1826*, ed. William H. Gilman,

Alfred R. Ferguson, and Merrell R. Davis (Cambridge: Belknap Press of Harvard Univ. Press, 1961), 27.

8. Cindy Dampier, "Mindfulness Is Not Just a Buzzword, It's a Multibillion Dollar Industry. Here's the Truth About the Hype," *Chicago Tribune*, July 2, 2018, https://www.chicagotribune.com/lifestyles/ct-life-debunking-mindfulness-0702-story.html.

9. Pierre Hadot, *The Inner Citadel: The "Meditations" of Marcus Aurelius* (Cambridge: Harvard Univ. Press, 1998), 124.

10. Emerson, *Journals and Miscellaneous Notebooks*, vol. 2, 28.

11. Pierre Teilhard de Chardin, *The Heart of Matter* (Lulu, 2016).

12. Saint Augustine, *Harvard Classics: Complete 51-Volume Anthology: The Greatest Works of World Literature* (e-artnow, 2019).

13. Hierocles, *Ethical Fragments* (Lulu, 2015), 53.

14. Epictetus, *The Art of Living* (Prabhat Prakashan, 2021).

BIBLIOGRAPHY

Aurelius, Marcus. *Meditations*. Trans. Gregory Hays. New York: Random House, 2002.

Baker, Carlos. *Emerson Among the Eccentrics*. London: Penguin, 1997.

Bode, Carl, and Malcolm Cowley, eds. *The Portable Emerson*. London: Penguin, 1979.

Emerson, Ralph Waldo. *Society and Solitude*. Delhi: Prabhat Prakashan Publishing, 2020.

———. *Letters and Social Aims*. South Yarra, Australia: Leopold Classic Library, 2016.

———. *Ralph Waldo Emerson Collection: Collected Essays and Lectures—Nature, The American Scholar, Essays: First and Second Series, Representative Men, The Conduct of Life, English Traits*. Independently published, 2022.

———. *On Man and God: Thoughts Collected from the Essays and Journals*. White Plains, NY: Peter Pauper Press, 1961.

———. *Uncollected Writings: Essays, Addresses, Poems, Reviews and Letters*. Madrid: HardPress Publishing, 2014.

———. *Selected Journals, 1841–1877*. New York: Library of America, 2010.

Epictetus. *Discourses and Selected Writing*. Scotts Valley, CA: CreateSpace Book Publishing, 2016.

Geldard, Richard. *The Spiritual Teachings of Ralph Waldo Emerson*. Hudson, New York: Lindisfarne Books, 2001.

Kazin, Alfred. *God and the American Writer*. New York: Vintage Books, 1998.

Porte, Joel, ed. *Emerson in His Journals*. Cambridge: Belknap Press of
    Harvard Univ. Press, 1982.

Porte, Joel. *Representative Man*. New York: Oxford Univ. Press, 1972.

Richardson, Robert D. *Emerson: The Mind on Fire*. Berkeley: Univ. of
    California Press, 1995.

Seneca. *Letters from a Stoic*. London: Penguin, 1969.

Thoreau, Henry David. *Walden*. Scotts Valley, CA: CreateSpace Book
    Publishing, 2018.

Wilson Allen, Gay. *Waldo Emerson*. London: Penguin, 1982.